Teachers as Counsellors

Alick Holden

TEACHERS AS
COUNSELLORS

Constable London

First published in 1969
by Constable & Co Ltd
10 Orange Street, London WC2H 7EG
Copyright © 1969 by Alick Holden

Reprinted 1973

ISBN 0 09 456430 2

D 533 8·80

Printed in Great Britain by
Redwood Press Limited
Trowbridge, Wiltshire

A teacher affects eternity; he can never tell where his influence stops.

HENRY ADAMS
The Education of Henry Adams

Flaming youth has become a flaming question. And youth comes to us wanting to know what we may propose to do about a society which hurts so many of them.

FRANKLIN D. ROOSEVELT
Address, 1936

Acknowledgements

M y serious interest in counselling was first aroused through being asked to work for the Marriage Guidance Council, but the views and opinions expressed in this book are, of course, purely personal and should not necessarily be regarded as those of the National Marriage Guidance Council, any of its affiliated councils or individual members.

It will, however, be apparent that I have been greatly influenced by the constructive thinking and action of the Council. Moreover, I am deeply indebted to it for the stimulus it has given me to think continuously about new patterns of school relationships, and the responsibilities which schools nowadays seem to have to assume. In particular I am extremely grateful to my friends and colleagues over the years in the Merseyside Marriage Guidance Council, not a few of them teachers, whose continuing critical appraisal of aims and methods has been accompanied by rare warmth, sincerity and tolerance. Above all I owe an inexpressible debt to my wife, my partner in so many excursions into the company of young people, not only for the partnership but also for her constant encouragement and help when I most needed them in the sometimes frustrating task of writing this. I should like to thank *New Society* for granting me permission to quote material from my article 'Teachers as Counsellors' which appeared on 23rd March 1967. Lastly I am most thankful for the many constructive suggestions which Miss Elfreda Powell has put forward, and for Miss Sheila Browne's untiring aid in the book's final stages.

A.H.

Contents

Introduction

This book is about personal counselling of adolescents in their schools. Its theme is that such counselling can be undertaken by some of the teachers in these schools. Its origin lies in experiences which have involved me in the personal lives of students in my own schools. They came to talk in confidence about their personal problems, attitudes and relationships, some of which seemed trivial, and others desperately serious. They were not invited to come and their confidences were not sought. There is no title 'Counsellor' on my office door. They were not given careers advice, psychological tests, psychiatric treatment or forms to complete, for their needs seemed urgent and time scarce. Their behaviour suggested that they would have been surprised, disappointed or frustrated, if any of these alternatives had been offered. My records are brief, informal and wholly confidential between them and me. They must have come because they felt they needed to talk to someone outside their family circle, because they needed a relationship with someone. Whether they were, and are, the 'tip of an iceberg', or a minority of unrepresentative young people, I do not know. The central fact is that I was a teacher in their school: it still surprises me that they came to talk to a schoolmaster.

These experiences have some bearing upon the current debate about counselling in schools, especially on the alleged conflict between the supposedly distinctive roles of authoritarian schoolmaster and co-operative counsellor, and on the ensuing contention that counsellors should be non-teaching specialists rather than teacher-counsellors part of whose time is devoted to orthodox teaching. As I see it, in the light of considerable experience

I

with individuals and groups in school and outside it, with every sort of client between the ages of fourteen and twenty-one, personal counselling entails one person, the counsellor, making a relationship with another, the client, so as to help the latter to come to terms with himself, to look sensibly at his situation, and thus come to the stage at which he is able to solve his own problems, including those which were the occasion of his visit to the counsellor, without the latter imposing his ideas upon the client. Those are the bare bones of the matter, and we shall see later that it can be a much more complex affair involving situations of considerable delicacy. Stated in these relatively simple terms, however, it is perhaps clear that this relationship is not an easy one for the conventional teacher to accept. It is, moreover, not only the teaching-counselling relationship which is complex, but also the implications which counselling by teachers in their own schools carries for the whole nexus of relationships within those schools; relationships with colleagues and the effect upon colleagues' relationships with their pupils are but two examples which spring readily to mind.

Beyond the confines of the school itself there are relationships with parents, with governing bodies and local authorities to be considered. We do not know with any degree of certainty how far parents are prepared to accept the idea that their children may blurt out in the privacy of the counselling room all sorts of domestic information, which may amount to social dynamite. Many people are increasingly irritated, to say the least, about the number of agencies which, in their view, 'snoop' upon what used to be the sacred privacy of family life, and it may be thought that the teacher-counsellor could become another of these agencies. Much must depend on the character of the counsellor, his sense of responsibility and his ability to co-operate, when necessary, with parents and others in dealing with personal problems that students bring to him. Clearly it is undesirable to foist upon our community yet another agency simply because someone thinks it is a good idea, without the need having been established or some thought given to it. My experience, however, suggests that the need exists, and others certainly have formed the same view.

Thus it is that the discussion about counselling in schools grows apace. The Schools Council has produced a Working Paper on the subject; the National Association for Mental Health has a working party which is reviewing counselling in schools; several universities and colleges* of education are running counselling courses, or courses which contain a counselling element. Some local authorities provide in-service training courses in counselling or Education in Personal Relations (known as EPR), an activity which can be the nursery of counselling situations. Increasing numbers of secondary schools have posts carrying specific welfare and pastoral responsibilities, which are occupied by teachers to whom children are encouraged to take their *personal* problems. And yet there is much uncertainty about the counsellors' true function, while teachers who occupy these posts are not always fully aware of what these non-teaching duties may involve or of how to cope with situations which arise out of them. There is also much confusion in the minds of teachers and other educationists about counselling itself.

'I have been doing this for years'; 'All teachers are counsellors'; 'I could not cope with that'; 'Of course teachers cannot be counsellors'; 'Teachers must counsel, we do not want outsiders in'; 'Counselling is a job for specialists': this sample of teachers' statements during and after a conference on counselling reveals uncertainty about counselling and differences of attitude to the teachers' tasks in the 1960s and 1970s. Teachers variously suspect that counselling is just another gimmick or stunt, new jargon for the sort of informal advice which some have always given to their students, or yet another burden thrust upon their weary backs by educational boffins far removed from the sombre realities of the class-room. On the other hand they sometimes look upon coun-

* A list of these is given in Appendix III.

selling, hopefully perhaps, as a subtle way of maintaining law and order, or as a new aspect of their task and providing a service to meet real need. The first three of these can be disregarded as topics for serious consideration here and I hope to show that while the last of them envelops the real meaning of counselling to which most of this book is devoted, it is avoiding an important issue not to consider counselling as an aid to what we, perhaps wrongly, call school discipline – perhaps harmony is a better word – especially at a time when traditional sanctions are under challenge. The functions are closely connected and cannot be divorced from the larger problem of the function of the teacher in present-day society, which is inevitably the implicit background of this book.

It seems to me that some teachers already have, or have the capacity to make, relationships with their students of such a quality that it should not be difficult for them to take the further step into the deeper experience of counselling through which the varied difficulties of adolescence become understandable and less disturbing. The use of the word 'quality' here presents difficulties: it is almost beyond definition, but, expressed in straightforward terms, in my view the relationship between teacher and student is poor when the latter is motivated by fear alone, that is the fear of consequences of any action at all on his part in work or other school activities, and the teacher controls solely by the use of threat of sanctions; when the teacher's image is wholly authoritarian and no element of mutual partnership exists. A teacher in this relationship is in no position to consider counselling, and may have difficulty in understanding those who can counsel. But even those who have an appropriate relationship, and view counselling favourably, are not always aware of the emotional stresses to which counselling may subject them, the delicacy of the situations in which they may become involved, or the compulsion which counselling exerts upon them to re-examine and re-orientate their professional attitudes and relationships within their schools. That this compulsion exists will, I hope, emerge during the book.

There are, of course, outside specialists who offer services which in the broad sense comprise counselling and with which teacher-counsellors in schools ought to be familiar. Notably these include Child Guidance and Mental Health organisations, with expert knowledge in their field of activity, which is beyond the capacity of a school teacher-counsellor. The teacher's great advantage is his first-hand knowledge of the students with whom he comes into contact. This is the possible embryo of a more personal relationship in which they could find it easier to talk with him than with a third party with whom the relationship is likely to be more formal. A teacher-counsellor ought, however, to be able to refer cases beyond his competence to these experts, and to know where they can be found.

The purpose of this book is to show that it is possible for a teacher to counsel in his own school despite the alleged duality of role and the conflict implied by this duality between the teacher with authority behind him and the counsellor operating with his client as a partner in a joint enterprise. It seeks to examine the counselling relationship and to outline the special problems which that relationship can create for a teacher who counsels in his own school. It indicates how one practising schoolmaster has approached solutions of the problems created by the dual role and makes some suggestions about organisation, selection and training for counselling. It is concerned with counselling in the school situation, and its view is commonsense rather than clinical. Counsellors working in different circumstances may, therefore, find it less profound and analytical than they believe the subject merits. I hope to encourage those who take a slightly jaundiced view of counselling not only to understand what it means and entails but also to examine the possibilities which it offers for educational advance even in traditional intellectual terms. This book may also urge to further efforts those teachers whose relationships with their students are already scarcely distinguishable from that between a counsellor and his client, relationships which they have achieved because they have personal qualities which make them acceptable to their youthful students. This group comprises those who are engaged in education in personal relationships, and ought to include others who have definitive pastoral responsibilities. Yet others may find it interesting and helpful; those who train teachers in colleges of education and university departments, or conduct in-service training in EPR and counselling; community service workers; health, welfare and probation officers; clergymen, and even parents.

The use of the masculine gender throughout is purely a matter of convenience, for counselling is as important to one sex as it is to the other, and frequently involves both.

I. The Nature of Personal Counselling

Careers guidance, psychological testing and scholastic advice, all of which come within the scope of counselling as it is described in the *Schools Council Working Paper*, have fairly definitive goals and well-organised techniques based upon considerable experience and knowledge. They are well documented elsewhere, most schools have careers experts and advisers about further education on the staff, while local education authorities have child guidance officers well acquainted with guidance techniques and testing methods. These fields of activity do not come within the purview of this book. Personal counselling is less well defined and there is little information yet available about its use in schools because there is a shortage of experience. The epithet 'personal' implies a wide range of situations with which a personal counsellor might have to deal, and this breadth implies some difficulty in framing precise rules and procedures. They may be undesirable anyway. Nonetheless some guidance is necessary to underline the importance of the attitudes, reactions and motives of the teacher-counsellor, as well as to suggest possible guiding principles.

An analysis of a single case offers a useful starting point from which to move into more general principles. That which I have chosen is unusual in the problem it presents, and the challenge it offers to the teacher's ability to switch roles from teaching to counselling. I had often chatted 'off the record' with the client before this particular occasion; by then he was nearly eighteen. In his earlier career there had been minor and not exceptional breaches of formal school discipline. Superficial investigation into these had revealed a vague pattern of disharmony at home.

Conversations with parents in school on rare occasions had proved abortive and the real causes of the earlier trouble had never been ascertained. By the age of sixteen he had begun to develop into a young man who had considerable strength of character, a sense of public service and the ability to read to advanced level. He and I had talked about his future prospects in academic and career terms, but never about the details of his personal life, and no hint had been given of the problem which the counselling now to be described uncovered. I have broken the record of the case into sections. At the end of each section there are notes intended to clarify the principles behind my attitude and approach to that section, as well as the client's reactions. These will, I hope, be helpful towards understanding the counselling experience. As other cases are reported in less detail near the end of this chapter, they are all numbered for ease of future reference. For disguise reasons certain details of this case and the cases at the end of the chapter have been slightly altered.

CASE I
Stage 1

The door of my room, which has a small adjoining office, opened behind me as I was gazing out of the window, just after the end of formal school. The door closed: I thought the school-cleaner had returned for something and did not turn round, but continued to think about tomorrow's practical work. Suddenly a deep voice behind me: 'Are you busy, sir?' The boy looked very pale and worried. I forgot about the view and the practical work.

'There is nothing that cannot wait. Do you want to talk?'

'Please. I'm in trouble or going to be. Perhaps I ought not to tell you – in any case there's nothing you can do.'

'We shall have to find out whether I can do anything. You are here. What is the trouble?'

'It's my girl friend.' Long pause. Then – and the words fairly tumbled out – 'It's not what you think.'

'Oh! What do I think?'

'I thought you'd think she was pregnant.'

'Why should you believe that was in my mind?'

'Most middle-aged people think that's the matter as soon as you mention girl friends and trouble.'

'We can talk about middle-aged people later, when we have had a look at your problem, but not now. Is she pregnant?'

'No.'

'Are you sure? I can help you if she is – or I know where she can get help. But if she is not then we do not have to worry about this, do we? What trouble are you in or going to be? This is what I want to know.'

'It's a long story, but she is going to be thrown out of her home and it is my fault.'

'I should like to hear the whole story. Tell it how you like. I shall treat whatever you have to say in complete confidence and disclose it to nobody unless you give your permission to do so to anyone who I might think could help me to assist you.'

Comment

By this time he had relaxed appreciably, and was in better control of himself, far from what I had originally thought was breaking point. His problem was unique among dozens of different problems presented by adolescents in school, and likely to be very complicated. The purpose of this first part of the interview, which had lasted about fifteen minutes, was to put him at his ease. There was no question that he was interfering with any work which I had to do, that it might for other reasons be inconvenient to talk with him at that moment. His nervously abrupt manner and his appearance were not important to me. His earlier school record, the misdemeanours and the occasionally erratic work – none of these was relevant to the central fact of the situation, that he was there and in some sort of trouble. In plain language

he had something to get off his chest. He wanted to talk to someone without being criticised or rebuked. Criticism and rebuke
might of course be justifiable but this was not important; his
feelings and problems at that moment were.

The first few sentences reveal his own uncertainty about approaching me. Perhaps he ought not to tell me, or I should be
unable to help because of my position, he might think; his remarks
about middle-aged people imply an expected reaction on my part
or are a safeguard against a possible rebuff. At this stage he needs
reassurance, not that I am going to agree with him, but that, at
least, I am going to listen. It was possible at this point that this was
all he expected from me; equally he may have hoped that I might
solve his as yet undisclosed problem. I use the word undisclosed
because the statement that his girl is going to be expelled from
home was certainly not the whole problem. My function therefore was to put him at ease, to give him confidence to tell his tale
as he wished. To have rebuffed him in any way would probably
have driven him away, and this in the long run might have
exposed the pair of them to greater hazards. Therefore, he was
accepted without any reservations or condition, without passing
any judgements. The first few minutes of quiet conversation
enabled him to overcome his own fear of rejection and to present
his situation with more care and clarity, with less nervousness and
apprehension. Whether merely talking about his problem would
suffice, or whether he might want me to play a more active role,
would emerge later. For the moment, accepting him as he was
was all-important.

Stage 2

He now knitted the tale together much more coherently than his
earlier demeanour had suggested was possible. The gist of it was
this: His parents had thrown him out of home because at the age of
sixteen they had thought that he ought to get a job and earn some
money. What was the point of 'A' levels when he had 'O' levels

and they had arranged a job for him which would provide good money? But he wanted to obtain a professional qualification. If he failed in this, or was slacking, his parents might have some justification for their limited and materialistic view of his situation. He had therefore gone to live with some relatives who at least were much more tolerant and understanding of his hopes and ambitions, even if they too could not fully grasp what he hoped to achieve. He had a week-end and holiday job, plus a maintenance grant, so that there was no financial problem. His great support in this enterprise was his girl friend whom he had known for two years. She too was reading for 'A' levels: she also was not at ease with her parents who disagreed with higher education and not earning money at sixteen plus. His view was that they had sustained one another and would continue to do so, because they had similar problems and were trying to reach upward together from a morass of home difficulties. She used to come to his room: they studied together and discussed their work as well as their problems. His relatives knew that they did this and had raised no objection. Her parents, on the other hand, now said it was his fault that she was indulging in these wild fancies about higher education, that he was leading her astray in every sense. They had forbidden her to see him any more. If she did she would be thrown out from home. They had set a deadline four days from the date of the interview. It was his fault that this situation had developed, yet the relationship with the girl was essential to him. He could not break it off. What was to be done?

Comment

The client has now presented the problem as he sees it. It is, of course, possible that it was a fabrication, but this is his starting point. There are a number of brief answers, of course. That he must break it off is one; but this is unacceptable to him. That they should both go back home is another equally repugnant or impossible remedy. He did not come to be told to do what he could not bring himself to do. Enforcement would be difficult anyway. So far he has told me much. Apart from a few questions put in the course of normal conversation to set the events he had recounted in their proper sequence or perspective he has done all the talking. He answered the questions clearly and confidently, and did not seem to think that they reflected on his honesty or integrity, and everything he said was consistent with the truth of his story. This was a sign that the relationship between us was developing, far enough, I hoped, to be able to withstand further and more searching questions. For it seemed necessary to find out more than he had told me. The appropriate enquiries might still drive him away, and the prospect of a sensible solution to his problem might disappear. The interview must therefore be continued with care.

Stage 3

There was silence for several minutes. This was certainly an unusual case. I said, 'Which school does she attend?' He told me.

'Has she talked to anyone on the staff at school about her situation?'

'You can't talk to schoolteachers!' The humour of this reply struck me forcibly, despite its vehemence, but before any reply could be made he apologised in great haste and confusion, several times.

I said, 'That is not important – at least compared with your situation. The point is that someone in her school would be in a better position to help her in lieu of her parents than I am. Have you suggested that she might talk to someone at school?'

He had not. She had never mentioned anyone on the staff who seemed to be willing to listen to student troubles. Asked about other relatives, there were none. I asked if he had any ideas of his own. 'We could live together,' he replied, looking me straight in the face.

'Certainly that is one solution to the problem. Since you have mentioned it let us discuss it. You will be able to share your troubles, to console and fortify one another in your struggles against the manifold difficulties with which you are beset. Both of you will feel that you will have a sympathetic atmosphere, away from the continued hostility of your parents. You have, at present, broken relations with your parents – for good, you feel. It is likely that if you both agree to embark upon the course you have suggested she will break completely with hers. Is this total severance of parental relations, on both sides, what you really want? You may regret it in the long run. Then again, consider her, alone. What happens to her if anything happens to you, or your partnership disintegrates? Does she go on the scrap-heap? My recollection is that males of your generation do not like other people's cast-off goods – at least they say this. There are also material considerations involved. What about money? And the equipment of a home – for that is what you wish to set up? There are certain harsh realities to be faced in this context. These are my immediate and very brief reactions to your suggestion, but I should like more time to think about the problem, although I know it is desperately urgent to you. Will you come and see me tomorrow, first thing?'

'Can we talk a little more now, please?' was the reply. 'I know where I can get a place to live, and I have offers of furniture and fittings from friends. We have looked at the money problem and we can manage.'

'Are you saying that you have made up your mind and simply want someone's blessing?'

'At least it is something we can do ourselves, and not be dependent on someone else.'

'Of course it is, and such independence and self-reliance does you credit. You have had some bitter experience of dependence upon adults who were unresponsive to your feelings and naturally want to be rid of them. But you have not answered the other problems I outlined. Do you want to dodge them?'

'She thinks as I do.'

'I should like to know what she thinks about the problems you have not dealt with. How far are you the dominant partner in the relationship, dictating policy as it were?'

'You don't know her. I don't think I could persuade her to do anything which she really disapproved of.'

'All right. Let us accept for the moment your joint agreement on this proposal of living together. You are prepared, in full awareness, it seems, of the consequences to her and her relations with her parents to go ahead and "burn your boats". You argue that her parents, like yours, have abandoned all their responsibilities, that therefore you have responsibilities for her and that your suggestion – living together – is the best way of discharging these. Not everyone would agree with you, but before following this up, what are your more long-term plans for the future? After leaving school? Both of you?'

'She already has a place in college. I think I shall get one.'

'In a few months' time therefore you are likely to separate and only see one another during vacations and odd week-ends, a total of one quarter of each of the next three years.'

'Yes – but that won't break us up.'

'Supposing the relationship does not survive this continuous interruption? What happens to her? You can go back to your relatives really, and some people think it matters less for a young man to be left on his own, even if they will not have you back. Where does she go if you break up?'

'This can't happen. We are too dependent upon one another.'

'I am sure you are, in the present unhappy state of affairs in which you are a solace and a comfort to one another, and a bar to great loneliness. But supposing either of you in the future met someone else for whom you cared. Would you then split up, or stay together out of loyalty simply because you lived together? We cannot foresee these situations but someone wrote that "Conduct is masterful administration of the unforeseen". Should you then burn your boats at this stage in your lives? There are other considerations for you to think about, too. Notwithstanding the expulsion of their daughter from home, her parents might try to invoke the law to protect her from what they think is your evil influence. She is a minor, you know. Also, living together as you suggest contains a considerable risk apart from any moral judgement; the arrival of a child could upset your plans, wreck your professional training – certainly hers. This could be the germ of much future recrimination when you looked back in later life at what you might have been, in moments of depression. I take it that you know what you are about in the purely sexual sense in your relationship?'

He nodded. They both knew, and later conversations confirmed this. He had not thought about the legal side of the matter, nor about possible future effects upon the relationship – in any case it was a bit difficult for him to see that far ahead, wasn't it? I went on.

'Of course it is hard for you in your present difficulties to look that far ahead, but I can only pass on to you the experience of seeing much misery caused by the sort of situation we are looking at. You do not have to take any notice of possibilities suggested by older people, but at least they have been passed on. The immediate problem, however, is the possibility of her being thrown out, for your course of action cannot be put into operation immediately. I can put you in touch and pave the way with people who are experts at this sort of situation. You can take the action. These people will ask questions and you should be able to answer them honestly. They may also make enquiries on their own, for they have responsibilities to their sponsors which they must discharge, as you feel you must yours.'

He departed. We met several times again and talked the problem over in greater detail.

Comment

The early stages of this are very ordinary: enquiries about home
and school and relatives; who could best help? His comment,
'You can't talk to schoolteachers', produced two interesting
reactions: on his part a fumbling desperate apology lest I should
withdraw in anger – a reaction which made me feel that he
wanted to continue the relationship and that his contribution to
it was stronger than I expected; and, on my part, a suppression of
genuine amusement for fear he would think I was ridiculing him.
This single incident largely removed any earlier feeling I had that
he would withdraw, a feeling confirmed by his insistence on continuing that evening. It enabled me also to be more direct and less
tentative in the subsequent discussion than I might otherwise have
been. Almost immediately he produced his solution to the problem – living with his girl friend. This proposal is, in one sense, the
test of the relationship between counsellor and client. He did not,
I think, expect me to agree with it but I do not know whether he
expected me to condemn it out of hand. As a counsellor I must
accept this solution, as I had earlier accepted him and his recital,
as a basis for rational discussion. Immediately a problem arises.
Should a teacher countenance such a suggestion? We shall have to
look at this as a principle in a later chapter, but when confronted
with the suggestion, made in good faith on the client's part, there
is no alternative to discussing it, apart from discarding it out of
hand, and the latter course would almost certainly have precipitated the client's withdrawal. In retrospect, I do not think I would
handle a similar case any differently. The counsellor's function at
this stage seemed to be to listen further, to pose questions which
the client has to answer, if he pursues the course which he proposes
himself; he can also contribute experience which an older person
can offer to a younger, and suggest possible consequences of the
suggested action; he can give practical information, not affected
by opinion or judgement, which is relevant to the immediate

problem. But he can only do this if he accepts the client, not only at the beginning but all through his statement; the constant tone of questions put to him was intended to accept him as well as to make him think and to extend his sense of responsibility to topics which he deliberately or unintentionally overlooked. At the back of both our thoughts there was, I think, always the lurking possibility that I might express some dogmatic assertion of moral principle, which would override in the client's mind the acceptance accorded to him, an acceptance which is crucial to the whole counselling operation, and must become an almost instinctive reaction on a counsellor's part.

The relationship between counsellor and client in this interview – the first of several – is different from that which most teachers would regard as usual between teacher and taught, even allowing for the relaxed informality which characterises relationships between some sixth-formers and some of their teachers. It is significant that earlier contact with this client had in fact not been appreciably different from that with his fellows in school; yet the counselling position originated there and demanded a change of role on the teacher's part, a change accepted, indeed expected, by the client. Clearly this young man is quite intelligent and specific details of the counselling approach in this instance might not be equally appropriate to a client who was younger or less intelligent. Considerations of age and intellect, however, should not blind us to the general principles of counselling as this interview exemplifies them or to the difficulties which the change of role presents to the teacher. Neither should one be diverted by the rather unusual circumstances of the case, for the counsellor's attitude is not altered by the particular complexity of any given case. Indeed its very complication illustrates what may be unearthed by a request for a few minutes' conversation, from which a counsellor cannot withdraw when he discovers that what he is told is not to his liking or is contrary to his principles. He has to be prepared by his own temperamental stability, and by technical knowledge and approach, to handle whatever comes to his hearing. No counsellor knows what his client will produce; he must be ready to accept anything. We can turn later to the difficulties offered by the teacher's change of role to counsellor, and to the problems of temperamental suitability. The immediate issues are the two general principles of counselling which this interview illustrates, and which are of overriding importance: acceptance and privacy.

ACCEPTANCE

From the information given in this case we can, of course, draw some conclusions about the youth involved. However, he was primarily worried, unhappy and upset. Other clients are angry and disturbed; there are as many states as there are clients. One cannot wish that one's clients were cool, calm and collected. If they were in this serene state they would either not need counselling, or counselling would be a less taxing matter. The immediate presenting situation is that, like this young client, they are not serene, and counselling practitioners have to take their clients as they are, or as they believe themselves to be. Certainly, they may have to find out why they are in these disturbed conditions as a part of the counselling process; but no counsellor can even begin to do this unless he accepts tacitly at the very start his clients' disturbed attitudes, their conduct, dress and other characteristics quite imperturbably. For this relaxed acceptance of the whole client is the nursery of a relationship between client and counsellor, in the security of which the client can begin to find his own calm and serenity. Being put at ease is the first step to peace of mind. In the client's mind, the counsellor is ready to give him time, patience and a friendly hearing; he is interested but not disturbed. In a school situation a student can think: 'This man is not bothered by my poor work record, or outbursts of indiscipline, he holds nothing against me, he takes me as I am: he is unhurried and unflurried.' This first client wanted time at the moment he asked for it, not a hasty, clock-watching reception;

quiet sympathy and understanding, not outraged condemnation; he wanted his ideas to be discussed rationally without moral judgement. The satisfaction of these needs was the prior condition for this troubled client to begin what is for anyone, especially an adolescent, the hard process of taking a grip of himself, not by orders which he cannot accept but by the slow and tenuous growth of his own self-control. Only then can he begin to 'state his case', and the counsellor's continued calmness through the statement maintains this progress until he reaches the point at which he can discuss his problems freely with the counsellor. The latter is always emotionally divorced from the client's situation, although concerned about it. This enables him to look at it more clearly and coolly than the client can. He can induce by his example rather than by imposition such an attitude in his client that the latter can, little by little, think more sensibly than he could when he was 'steamed up' by his situation. One cannot say to a client – I could not have said it to this first one – 'Pull yourself together!'. People go to counsellors because this is what they cannot do. Clients do not want an emotional reaction from a counsellor, whether it stems from questioning his beliefs or challenge to his supposed position and authority. If they do receive this, they react in turn against him and the potential partnership dissolves into angry and futile confrontation. Calm acceptance and relaxed demeanour are the counsellor's first remedies for a disturbed client.

Now teachers are accustomed to giving advice, guidance and instructions to students, often with good humour and patient kindness, but behind the relationship there is always an element of authority. For this reason, I have possibly laboured the idea of acceptance. The acceptance relationship contains no element of authority whatsoever, and here lies the central difficulty in principle and practice for the teacher who counsels – the unconditional abandonment of his authoritarian role as a teacher without which counselling is impossible. One is also confronted with the further difficulty that many adolescents do not believe that it is possible for a member of a school staff to play two such different roles, certainly at the present stage in the growth of school counselling, but before his client can accept this, it falls upon the teacher-counsellor to accept the dual function, to adjust to and live with it.

Acceptance is sometimes confused with agreement. A later development of the interview described throws light on this. After the first meetings I saw the client I have mentioned several times. Quite early in these subsequent discussions he asked outright whether I agreed with his proposals. I did not answer him at first, but asked whether my view was at all important to him, for it seemed to me that he did not care whether anyone agreed with him or not – an attitude which I accepted. He replied that he had his views, but he would like to know mine. Now it is very easy for me looking at his situation from the outside to disagree with him, but I told him that I would not recommend his course of action to anyone, whether they were in his predicament or not, and outlined my views on monogamous marriage and extra-marital intercourse, views which were largely a matter of personal faith about the value of human beings. We discussed the differences between us at some length. The essence of this, however, is that my views were given at his prompting, not by my dictation, and they were sought presumably when he felt the relationship was strong enough to survive this fundamental disagreement. Case 3 later on (p. 43) illustrates this in a different context, in which the four clients accepted my standpoint after I had accepted theirs. No one compromises his own principles by counselling, and while generalisation is dangerous it may be doubtful whether anyone can counsel adequately, especially in difficult cases, without a basis of personal principle which is a course of stability in challenging situations. But it is not a counsellor's function to impose his personal faith and principles upon others. I discuss this further in Chapter IV.

At a less exalted level perhaps, and in settings different from the counselling room, adults who love classical music but detest 'pop' songs can accept adolescents' admirations of those who top the popular 'Hit Parade'. Some teachers find it possible to exploit this and to apply that taste to more 'classical' musical menus. Enlightened teachers of English have used their pupils' enjoyment of comics, thrillers and popular serials to acquire a similar appreciation of a different literary genre. Similarly, it has been shown that some useful mathematical knowledge can be acquired from a study of playing cards and football league tables. All these examples illustrate the benefit to be gained by accepting the students' position as it is, and using it to move on to different, more general or sophisticated ideas. They start with the pupil as he or she is, not where they might like them to be. Yet each category of teachers involved in these subjects has some other standard to which they seek to lead their pupils, even if it is only to an awareness that what the pupils know from their own limited experience is incomplete and inadequate for their future development. It is but a step to extrapolate this into matters of human relationship and social conduct, but a teacher-counsellor must first understand this extrapolation in his own mind.

PRIVACY

Privacy for the counselling interview is essential. It must be accompanied by the undertaking given to the client in the first case not to disclose what was said without his permission. This undertaking was unconditional and its purpose is to enable the client to explain his whole predicament, without fear of disclosure to anyone. He must be able to see his position thus: 'This man will not tell anyone what he has heard; he sees me as a person as himself, not as the representative of an agency or organisation, e.g. the school staff or the governors, who might take action, after he has reported to them, without my agreement; he will not publish any records; he is not concerned about his position, but only about me.' Any client gains confidence from this environment. The situation which the first client disclosed was serious. As he described it, I could not handle it alone; specialised help was necessary, and I knew where it could be obtained. It can be alarming to encounter such a situation, and a counsellor, in good faith and in the client's best interests, must judge when he should refer the client's problem to some other person or agency. If the client agrees, as he did in the example, there is no problem. If he does not, the counsellor can do nothing, except continue counselling. The bond of confidence given in privacy must not be broken, however irrational the wishes of the client seem to be. The relationship between client and counsellor is based on mutual trust and acceptance: in school the age difference between client and counsellor accentuates the responsibility of the latter to keep his word. If he breaks it, he not only destroys the personal rapport between them, but he may also exacerbate the general lack of communication between his client and the whole older generation, whose representative, the counsellor, has demonstrated how unreliable they are. Moreover, he has shown that he cannot accept his client as he is, for if he had done he would not have broken his own solemn promise of privacy.

Many people confronted with the first case would wish to 'do something' out of sheer helpfulness, but a counsellor's task is to help his client to reach the point at which the latter can accept what seems to be in his best interests in the light of the counsellor's experience. This is not just a device to be helpful, still less to unload the client on to someone else whom he does not know and may resent. It is rather a part of helping the client to come to terms with his situation and to face realities, not to avoid it or to pretend they do not exist. When he has reached this stage he can accept also the idea that other people can be more useful than the counsellor, and be just as discreet. If this seems likely to be an alarmingly long business, my experience is that two or three interviews have usually been enough to establish sufficient trust and good faith with clients to enable them to accept guidance from agencies outside the counselling room.

So much for the basic conditions or principles of counselling; but there must be more to it than mere acceptance and private confidence. What does it achieve? How does it start and develop? How does it end? It is convenient, if arbitrary, to answer these questions under four headings: Aims, Beginning, Development, and Ending.

AIMS

Relaxed private chats with adolescents are pleasant. They can also be pointless. It is obviously a different story if a client asks for specific advice about careers or choice of subjects. There is an end in view in discussing these. Yet personal counselling could conceivably become a time-wasting exercise unless we can highlight possible benefits to a client, and to his school. Little is known about this. What experience there is is limited and scarcely measurable in terms of objective results. It is true that some students abandon slack work and misconduct as a result of counselling, but this is not its prescriptive aim. It can also solve specific problems for clients because the counsellor deploys his knowledge and experience on the client's behalf in such a way that the client accepts them because the counsellor has accepted him. But the central aim of counselling in school is more fundamental than just correcting misconduct and solving specific problems, although it includes these. It is to help the adolescent to understand himself, and the way he feels about other people and situations about which he seeks advice; to help him escape from a world of his own and face facts as they are, not as he might prefer them to be; to develop his own resources for coping with and adjusting to other people and situations. Much comment from adolescents in every walk of life suggests that personal

c

harmonisation of this kind is one process for which education and other social agencies make little provision at present. Tolerating patiently and understandingly angry complaints and personal stress in private is the beginning of adolescent movement into calmer waters of self-control and social integration without loss of individuality or personal opinion. A counsellor's cool acceptance and explanation of adolescent disturbance turns it into an understandable stage of human growth for those who experience it; the usual defensive reaction of the adult world can be seen as less oppressive: both disturbance and reaction cease to be the occasion for an unhealthy conflict between generations. Appropriately used, counselling can help to turn the whole educational process into a partnership between teacher and taught instead of that species of internecine warfare in which both parties suffer heavy casualties and society loses precious talent. It has another product too; it reveals the depth of character and intensity of feeling in quiet youngsters who commonly confine disturbance within themselves rather than expose themselves to criticism or ridicule by public utterance in class. The simple fact that one adult can take a youngster's feelings seriously enough to listen is often sufficient to enhance his self-control and to relax him out of his fears and tensions. To know that an adult can accept criticism rationally and talk about it is a salutary experience for many adolescents, and enables them in turn to accept adult comment as something worth listening to. This contribution to personal growth and maturation which counselling can make far outvalues its more obvious achievements, even when it exposes, as it can, family problems which lie hidden behind poor work, bravado and aggressiveness and which no amount of more conventional pastoral care ever completely reveals.

BEGINNING

How counselling starts, as it must do with the client making the voluntary decision to come, is still a mystery, and its development an art. Who on earth would take his troubles to a schoolteacher? Only clients can answer this. They seem to come, in small spates, followed by periods of quiet. One can only make intelligent speculations about the origin of their decision.

Every teacher has a reputation which comprises part of the folklore and legend of any school. Reputation covers a multitude of staff virtues and vices, characteristics and idiosyncrasies, but something in a particular person must lead students to seek his counsel. Perhaps he is known to be a good listener, or displays a real interest in and ability to communicate with young people whoever they are: he may give an impression of poise. stability and maturity. He may seem to be wise or sensitive, understanding or imperturbable, patient or kind, firm or just. Perhaps he portrays dignity without pomposity, is perceptive without being critical, implying that he has no reservations about people and never holds things against them. These and other facets of a teacher's character are the essential preconditions for the growth of confidence and harmony between him and his clients. These are all components of the inner man; yet external appearances have something to do with the decision to seek counsel. Student clients do not, I think, favour the 'with it' person as a counsellor. Adolescents will say that the adult who tries to identify himself with them in dress and manner has not himself grown up, that he has not accepted himself and the differences between him and his clients. Moreover, to say 'When I was young' in hearty agreement with an adolescent is to invite contempt. The client is interested in *his* youth and social climate, not the counsellor's.

Marriage and other adult counsellors are total strangers to their clients when they take up their first appointments. If a client does not like his counsellor he need not come again, and no harm will be done. But the teacher-counsellor is in a different position; he will see his clients round school and have professional influence on their futures. The clients-to-be are thus very chary of committing themselves into the hands of such an omnipresent person.

Consulting a teacher-counsellor is a step of great consequence therefore and they need to be sure of their man and perhaps personally upset as well, before they take it. These two factors induce the first approach. So they make up their minds, amid conflicting emotions, in loneliness and confusion, replete with the uncertainty of their age, to talk to someone who is older, but not prejudiced. They knock at the door: 'Can I see you for a few minutes?' They have initiated the experience, committed themselves to an adult, whom they believe they can trust.

DEVELOPMENT

The development of a counselling interview or a series of interviews varies from case to case. In general it is at best only possible to suggest guide lines and pitfalls rather than specify technique of universal applicability.

Notwithstanding what I have said before about teachers' reputations, the relationship between client and counsellor is extremely frail at the outset, and it is the latter's demeanour and attitude in the opening minutes which determine its development. There is no set formula of words which will of itself cement the bond between the intending partners, a bond which will enable them to move together into an area of what might be called more positive counselling, into joint exploration of the client's problems and attitudes. And, of course, this further enterprise is sometimes unnecessary, simply because the fact of talking to someone enables the client to go away and cope with life on his own. Such a simple outcome for the counsellor is nonetheless as valuable to the client concerned as more prolonged counselling might be to another: that the counsellor plays such a relatively small part is of no consequence. Such a client does not come again, but let us consider the client who stays, so that the counsellor must go further. He must explore with the utmost care his client's presenting situation, for the slightest, unintended implication that he is trying to impose on the client a solution to the presented difficulties will tend to drive the client away, because any such solution is quite unacceptable, at least in the early stages. If the client begins to react in this way, the counsellor has to start at the beginning again, accept the client's tale all over again, and abstain from the slightest hint that he is telling his visitor what to do. Even if this suspicion is apparently banished, the counsellor has constantly to fortify the relationship by referring back to what his client has said as an indication of his interest in and concern for him.

Counselling also becomes delicate when the counsellor's view of his client's situation and problems begins to form and does not coincide with the client's. Because he is not implicated emotionally, a counsellor can elicit a clearer view of what lies behind the situation presented to him. If at this stage there is trust between them, the counsellor can begin to discuss the situation, and the client will go along with him: if trust is not yet fortified sufficiently, the younger person will cast aside any opinion which the older may hazard; especially is this true when a teacher counsels a student. For here the young man may not only exhibit the normal quick hostility reaction of the adolescent, but also suspect that the teacher-counsellor will revert to the archetype of the teacher, the authoritarian *alter ego*. The relationship in such a case will revert to that of student-teacher, and the counselling connection disappear. The special circumstances in which a teacher counsels postulate that he is always on a razor's edge: there is always another view of him available to the client and he has only his own sympathetic interest, persistent acceptance and proof of privacy to ensure that this other pedagogic view of him does not reassert itself in the client's mind.

Suppose, for example, that the counsellor mentions a course of action which is relevant to the client's problems. The client says, 'I don't like that'. A sharp retort, 'Why not?', from the counsellor is quite inappropriate, for the client in turn reacts by thinking: 'This chap is no use to me: he has thought of something and as far as he is concerned that is the end of it; he has not begun to wonder

why I do not like what he says. He is beginning to play the
teacher again.' To him it looks as if the counsellor is trying to force
something upon him and we have seen that there is both a great
temptation for a teacher to do this and for the client to expect it
from a teacher. The course of action is unacceptable to the client
whether it is actually appropriate or not. The counsellor's wiser
approach is to say quietly: 'You may have thought of something
else', or 'Let us look at other ideas'. Each situation has to be played
'by ear', the counsellor always alert to signs of sudden tension in
the client's manner, which he must try to reduce. There may be
special reasons for a client's sharp and emotional reaction, of
which the counsellor will at first be unaware. A client might react
to the question 'Do you talk to your father?' by facial hardening
and a bitter 'No!'. The reaction implies disharmony between
father and son, which the client resents. Here 'Why don't you?'
by the counsellor might put the client in a difficult position. He
may wish to talk with his father, but the latter takes no apparent
interest, and the son may be unwilling to admit this apparent
defect in his parent. The counsellor might find an indirect approach more helpful. To whom does the client talk? Why that
choice? Are his friends in a similar position? A step at a time the
counsellor can lead his client to look at the reasons for his father's
attitude, and to accept them, or to find the strength to take some
initiative which the father might welcome or to survive the
father's rejection of it if this occurs. It may turn out that the
apparently strained relations between father and son were the
cause of the client's visit, although masquerading under some
nominal excuse. Whatever course the counselling takes, it is
intended to lead to the client understanding why he reacts in the
way he does, to encourage him to talk with increasing frankness
and with the counsellor's help and patience to accept situations
which he had rejected, for this is the first step towards dealing
with them. Adolescent clients have little experience of their own
on which to draw, whereas the counsellor has much. Such clients

are sensitive about this and resent treatment they believe is appropriate to infants by an adult who tends in their view to become overbearing and condescending. The examples quoted later in this chapter may help to understand a little of the art of the counselling approach, and some readers may recognise situations which have occurred in their own experience.

Exponents of non-directive counselling believe that counselling's sole purpose is to have the client understand and live with himself and his situations, the counsellor acting as a catalyst, but not working towards any specific goal, about which the counsellor may have a relevant opinion or prescriptive advice. All counselling has an element of non-directiveness and the later Cases 4 (p. 46) and 5 (p. 49) are entirely non-directive in the sense not of solving a specific problem but of helping the clients to sustain themselves. My own experience suggests that this is by no means true of all cases, some of which require a period of non-directiveness simply to establish a relationship, after which the special problems of the case can be studied jointly. Clients do appear who cannot accept any guidance, and others come post-haste every time they run into difficulty; these are the subjects of classic non-directive counselling in which the counsellor has to turn the client's attention to why he cannot cope with his difficulties, and why these exist, because no specific problem can be solved without understanding why he cannot cope and why they exist. Such a process, continued for some time, involves counsellor and client in a deeply therapeutic relationship. Many teachers who are prepared to accept the basic principles of counselling may feel that such a deep involvement with a client is beyond their temperamental resources, or entails an expenditure of time and deeper understanding of human psychology than they can contemplate, and that such cases should be referred to clinical psychologists or psychiatrists. Clearly teachers who counsel should know where such specialist help can be obtained. Cases as difficult as these I believe to be rare, and no teacher should be deterred from counselling by an impression that every student who comes to him is mad or seriously disturbed and needs deep psychiatric treatment. For it is remarkable how therapeutic the counsellor's relationship can be by itself, or seems to be. Loneliness, especially of adolescents, is perhaps the endemic malady of our time and society, and merely being able to talk to someone without restriction of any kind in a sort of community of mind or spirit so often provides the client with the resources to face life as it is, without any esoteric remedy or clinical technique being supplied by the counsellor, other than his transparent concern and interest. Those who advocate a more sophisticated and long-term expertise should not disregard the effect upon an adolescent of realising that behind the counsellor's attitude lies a caring mind, not an impersonal technique.

This brings me to the assumption which lies at the root of every sort of personal counselling: that the counsellor believes his clients have within themselves the ability to understand their difficulties and the underlying character to work out, with or without any explicit help from him, solutions to their own problems in something better than self-indulgent or pleasure-seeking terms alone. It is arguable that this is beyond the limits of adolescent resources, when rapid growth and physiological turbulence bring in their train oscillating attitudes and fluctuations in conduct. A counsellor ought to be able to explain these phenomena to his client as a contribution to self-understanding; for, despite a growing interest in sex education, the behavioural and emotional consequences of puberty are not easily understood, by adults or by the adolescents themselves, unless counselling and discursive approaches are used in dealing with them, rather than purely instructional. All this apart, however, there are sixteen-year-olds who are capable of the requisite self-examination and understanding, and for whom some non-directive counselling is extremely useful as a sorting-out process in which they simply think aloud to someone older, in private and without the emotional involvement which so often characterises discussions with their parents. Some teachers accept that this kind of counselling is comprehensible for intelligent students, but that it is not possible to apply to duller or younger students approaches which are relevant only for sixth-formers. Age and school status are not, I think, the significant criteria. We cannot make hard and fast distinctions without experiencing the reactions of a particular client, and deciding in the light of his reactions which development of counselling suits him best. Two considerations are important here. The first is that counsellors must adjust their choice of words to the literacy of their clients, for it is too easy to reject someone simply and solely because his vocabulary is limited. The second is a quite widespread belief that counselling is superfluous for bright sixth-formers. The extent of student breakdown in further education and the start of counselling services at this level rather suggests the contrary, and more student counselling in sixth forms when examination pressures are extremely severe might well prevent some of the breakdown which demonstrably occurs later on. Personal needs in my experience bear no relation to academic achievement, and some of our exam-crammed products often display a lack of personal balance which is comparable with that of the traditional delinquent.

At the back of most teachers' minds there must, I suspect, still lurk a pressing question. Even if they accept the ideas and methods of counselling, surely there must be a limit to which they can go in talking with their students. There must come a point at which they have to say to the client in effect, 'I have talked with you for a long time; you have done nothing but blame other people, circumstances and society for your predicament. Is it not time that you began to look at the sort of person you are? Why do you find it so difficult to stop grumbling about the talents others have? Why do you not try to use what you have instead? Is it not time you began to face the fact that you live in this society as it is, that it is impossible for you to deny its existence, to go on pretending that it is not there? You seek the benefits of the community, the food and services that are provided by the efforts of others, who may well be in the same sort of difficulty as you, but face up to it.' There is no set of rules which defines the point at which the counsellor says this or something like it: it is a matter for the counsellor's judgement alone. But if and when he does this, the counsellor must not do it in a fit of emotional exasperation or exhaustion, but in full and calm awareness of what he is doing. It is not to be done often, for it can be tantamount to a rejection of the client: a counsellor, if he takes this drastic step, writes off his client and himself, or runs the risk of so doing. For if the client cannot accept this kind of statement, he departs and the relationship ceases. In a sense, this question is connected with the problem of school discipline – to which I return later – but not only with that: it can be used deliberately in an attempt to bring the client up with a jerk, to help him to realise that even the counsellor has some limits beyond which he will not go. I have used it rarely, because it has rarely been necessary. Only one client departed in obvious anger and never spoke to me again. The three or four others responded by revising their attitudes and discussing their situations much more realistically. Such a reaction to a counsellor's criticism is, I think, explicable because the challenge is made against a background of a relationship in which the adult counsellor has established his good faith and patience, and is not just reprimanding the client in anger at some misdemeanour. If a counsellor uses this approach at the beginning of the first interview he is not even trying to counsel; when he uses it after several interviews he has shown that he is patient and concerned about his client, who can no longer blame the counsellor for his own failings.

If a client asks voluntarily for information or advice, it should be given. In a counselling setting the client knows that the counsellor is looking at the client's interests, not his own or the school's. The student who says 'You know what this [his problem] is all about, what do you think in the light of your knowledge and experience is the best thing for me to do?' assumes that the counsellor will answer him in good faith. The emotional temperature is low and the client has the option of accepting or rejecting the reply, without rancour. Given these conditions, to disregard the skill and knowledge which many teachers possess simply to maintain a façade of non-directiveness is scarcely sensible. Indeed, continuation of this can drive a young client away in frustration at the counsellor's apparent inadequacy. At this stage another benefit of the counselling relationship emerges. The client trusts the counsellor, certainly by the time the former is asking the latter for his opinion; if the school setting is right – and I suggest elsewhere in this book how this might be accomplished – the counsellor is also trusted by his colleagues on the staff. He is therefore in a position to act as a middleman between colleagues who could provide better advice than he can give and students who, even in these enlightened days, might be reluctant to approach them – why they should be thus reluctant does not concern us here, only the fact that this is the student's attitude. 'Would you like a chat with the careers expert? Why not go and talk to Mr X – he can give you sounder information about draughtsmanship than I? Mr Y knows more about the kind of help you want than I do: he has all the current information – go and see him.' A student may be confident about his relationship with the counsellor, but very uncertain of his reception at the hands of others, who are just other teachers to him: although he may think that the advice to seek out someone else is sound enough, he may not be able to bring himself to take it. One sees this written in the faces of clients when the suggestion to go elsewhere is made: they may even feel that the counsellor is rejecting them because he has had too much of them. This must be dispelled.

There are three possible answers here. The first is to ask the client who else on the staff he thinks he could talk to, about, for example, what subjects he should be studying, or what choices he should make. If he mentions someone in particular, let him go and talk with that person, trying to make the approach on his own, without the counsellor's direct help. The second is to suggest a specific person and ask the client if he would like an introduction in the form of a note. In this case the client is being encouraged to make his own approaches to another member of the staff, buttressed by the counsellor's note. The third, if the client really appears reluctant to do anything himself, is to offer to pave the way by having a preliminary talk with the staff colleague about the particular student who would like to come and see him, and to agree a suitable time. This virtually commits the client: he cannot fail to turn up at the appointed time without breaking faith with the counsellor. In practice I find the first method is the most widely used, and the third the least. The fact of being accepted by the counsellor, who be it remembered is also a teacher, seems to strengthen clients' resolve to take their own initiatives. I always tell students who turn to colleagues on my advice to come back to me if they want to discuss further what information they have gained from my colleagues, or indeed anything else. Some do, some do not: the latter presumably have found out what they want, or have made an equally significant relationship with a colleague, and this is all to the good from every point of view.

The stage has now been reached where the counsellor's job is virtually ended. His initial acceptance has given the client confidence, reassured him, made him capable of beginning to sort out his own problems. I mentioned that clients often do not return once they have begun to act on their own. Sometimes there is almost an extension of this, for I have had clients who, after talking with great freedom, and then departing, have been almost reluctant to talk with me again in any capacity for some weeks. I have never asked why this is so. It is almost as if they have some kind of near-resentment at having talked so freely and emotionally; they must also have wondered whether they had been wise in talking thus, whether their confidence had in fact been misplaced. Perhaps they were waiting for my reaction. After a time however they have come back, presumably when they have satisfied themselves that their doubts were unjustified, and that my attitude to them was not changed in public, but I have always left them to return without any prompting. Any private change in my attitude is always due to understanding them better as a result of counselling.

In this field of staff-student co-operation the counsellor's scope is enormous, and it conceivably extends also to education-related services, like the Youth Employment, School Welfare, and Medical Services. In the end it may be possible to extend it to improving home-relationships, by enhancing co-operation with parents; but this is a longer-term prospect, although I am certain that bolstering family stability wherever possible ought to be one of the indirect aims of counselling, possibly with the help of some-one on the staff who is interested in home visiting. Here, there-fore, we are moving into the field of team guidance and counsel-ling, but the foundation of it all, I believe, lies in the strength and meaning of the personal relationship between counsellor and client through which he becomes able to accept further guidance, or to act responsibly on his own.

ENDING

The only person who knows when counselling is finished is the client as a general rule, although some clients seem to feel they ought to keep coming until they are told not to – an odd hang-over from the teacher-student relationship. 'May I come again if I wish?' The dialogue is in this case clearly over, at least for the time being. The client may simply say 'Thank you' and go, with-out indicating whether he wants to return or not. On the face of things, this may seem offhand, but not all clients are accomplished in elegant manners. All that matters is that the door of the coun-sellor's room must be left open for a return in the future, perhaps not next week, but in a month or so. After two or three talks within a single week it is no bad thing to say to a client, 'We have discussed your problems quite fully. Would you like to go away and think about them on your own? If you want to come again, I shall be pleased to see you in a week or two. Leave it longer if you like, but remember I am available if you want to talk again.' Perhaps the client will come back two or three weeks later, and then leave for a longer period. In this way he is nursed into independence, and needs no further conversation. And sometimes, on the day he leaves the school, a client says, 'Goodbye – and thanks for the time you gave.'

Clearly counselling is an intricate business, very much a matter of judgement, especially in development after the delicate starting period of acceptance. Much depends on timing, and on the counsellor's assessment of his client. In schools and in general, a co-operative approach to the client's problems emerges when client and counsellor are in relaxed harmony, talking as equals, and the client availing himself of the greater experience of the counsellor, as and when he wishes. Whatever solutions may be reached, the client tends to think they are his own, and he may not recognise the counsellor's contribution. Teachers do find professional enjoyment in discussion with students on a person-to-person basis, and my impression is that students find it rewarding too as long as their status as people is admitted. Thus to extend discussion about study and jobs into more personal fields does not seem to be quite as great a step as some teachers think.

The following pages contain some examples of cases. The clients range from IQ 93 (at eleven plus) to IQ 132. I looked these figures up for interest only, not because they mean anything, for the ultimate destinations of these clients, or those to which they were heading, appear unrelated to these mystical figures. Neither are the patterns of counselling related to IQ. The clients were all young men, therefore, from the middle IQ range slightly tilted towards the top, and thoroughly representative in my teaching experience of students in the top halves of secondary modern schools and the lower streams of selective schools, and of streams four to seven in an eight-stream entry comprehensive school. 'Stream' here is simply a term of convenience to orientate the examples. The setting and introduction were common to all.

Some knocked on the door of my office, others approached me, rather furtively I thought, in the corridor. 'Can I see you for a few minutes, please?' was the universal opener. Sometimes I saw them immediately; for others I made appointments at mutually convenient times. Occasionally I would see seniors in their free periods. No one has ever failed to keep an appointment. I cannot recount with accuracy the atmosphere of their several verbatim tales and styles, but they ranged from the angry incoherence of fourth-formers to the elegant articulacy of sixth-form students. Each case is interspersed with notes reflecting briefly my reactions at the appropriate point, and is preceded by brief notes on character and reputation as it appeared to be known in the school before the interviews. This I always collected from the usual school sources as soon as a client had been to me for the first time. I call them cases, not to imply abnormality, but because this is the conventional term of the social case-worker, and there is no better.

CASE 2

> Pleasant well-built youth, sixteen: rather dim, but industrious without success; asks questions which 'any first-form boy could answer'; played no games, had no confidence and did not mix with his school-mates; little drive, but exceptionally courteous; I had taught him early in his school life, but did not think any relationship existed between us and his visit was a great surprise.

'I don't know where to begin, whether it is anything to do with you and you probably can't help anyway.' It is strange how often this last phrase occurs. He stopped, desperately near to tears. The first confidence had given way. We both sat in the strange silence which comes upon any school when the formal day's work is done.

There is a temptation at such a juncture to rush in and prompt the client. 'If you smoke and silence comes in the interview, blow smoke rings and wait', was the advice given by one experienced worker in the criminal counselling field; 'Give the youngsters a chance to relax by seeming to be relaxed yourself. No use saying "Come on, lad, what is it all about?"' Accepting the silence was part of accepting him. I do not know how long I should have waited if he had continued his reticence, but in the event he spoke again after only a minute or two during which he regained his composure.

'Have you a family of your own?' An unexpected question, this.

All sorts of ideas go through one's head when this happens. 'What on earth has my family got to do with his problems? He did not come here to ask about my family.' The one thing not to do is allow an emotional reaction like 'What business is it of his?'. He has asked the question. Perhaps there is a clue or lead in it.

'Yes.'
'Do you let them stay out late much?'

A hint of a problem here; important not to jump to a wrong conclusion and wreck his tentative probing by a comment or question which suggested I had decided on the hitherto flimsy evidence what his problem was. He is seeking my reactions; must reassure him by answering conversationally.

'My three are aged fifteen, twelve, and ten and still in the stage of being taken out as a family, although the eldest is showing signs of independent activity, and occasionally goes out with her friends. I like to know where she goes, with whom, and when to expect her back. The other two go to Scouts and Brownies and we know where they are and for how long.'

'Do you put a time limit on – especially for the eldest?'

Client is still probing my reactions really, sounding me out, perhaps comparing my views with someone else's. His story will come later. I am less sure of what it is – except that it is a family problem.

'It all depends on where she is going. If she is going to a friend's house we are prepared to make it eleven o'clock or eleven-thirty on special occasions if we know she will be brought home or can be called for. The important thing to us is knowing where she is and what she is doing. We have to trust them more and more as they grow older.'

He now took over the conversation; presumably the frank answers about my own family, without inhibition, gave him some confidence.

He was the laughing stock of his form and others outside because he had to be in by nine o'clock whereas most others seemed to be able to stay out until ten or eleven without any question. His contemporaries would have nothing to do with him because he could not do what they did. They had stopped inviting him to do anything. He resented their ridicule because many of them seemed to take no notice at all of their parents whereas he was suffering because he took notice of his. He was now sensitively angry.

Problem: he cannot stay out late. But why? Better for him to tell without prompting.

The prohibition also applied to church youth activities. The people he liked attended this church: sometimes a minister or lay official would ask young people to help at a function which went on later than nine o'clock. Because he could not stay, or could not go at all, the church too was beginning to think he was rather an odd character. He never told them why.

This certainly sounded weird. One does not generally meet objections to people attending church functions, which are usually well conducted. This is an objection to staying out late in general, not to particular activities. Why? No trust at all?

D

The case is far removed from school now. Yet if we can get to the bottom of it, perhaps his formal school performance will improve. Perhaps his frailty here is due to his preoccupation with parental problems like this.

I asked whether his parents took any interest in the church. His father did. There was no mention of mother.

Oh dear! Not a matrimonial case. There are snags in being a marriage counsellor. One tends to look for this kind of thing everywhere if one is not careful. I decided to plunge in and hope that the relationship between us was strong enough to stand it.

'And your mother?'

'My mother is an invalid and can hardly leave her bed, let alone the house.' The floodgates of venom opened and vitriolically he described the situation at home. Mother had been an invalid almost from the time of his birth he believed. She did little in the house, except grumble at his father who ran the home as well as a full-time job, without complaining at all. He was a saint who had to put up with an enormous amount of complaint from the mother. Mother was extremely suspicious of everything her son did, and father had to act so often as a cushion between them, justifying everything in which his son was interested. His concluding remark was quite savage:

'I know my mother is ill, but I don't think she tries as she might, and she is driving me and my father mad.'

I told him he might feel better for having talked about this, and invited him to come again.

I wanted time to think; we had spent almost an hour already. There is much in this counselling problem, some of it more relevant to the father's than the client's needs. It illustrates the social dynamite which can be exposed by a teacher who counsels. Every school ought to have this kind of information about its students, because in responsible hands it can help enormously in understanding and doing the best for students. But it is not the sort of data which everyone would like to think was being bandied about the staff-room. Immediate problem is how to help client in overcoming or living with the situation.

He came a few days later and we talked about why his mother felt the way she did. Perhaps she felt insecure or jealous because her illness made her so dependent on other people. I found out which church he attended. Had anyone from church been to their home and if so what had happened? No one had been probably because no one knew how difficult their situation was. I seemed to be the only person acquainted with the situation outside the three of them in the family.

I could involve myself with his family. I was reluctant to do this. A visit from a schoolmaster might make the mother wonder what was going on. I did not want to be a prop for them either; if I retired in the future from such a supporting role they might be worse off. There was also the time factor. It seemed to me that his church might be a better aid. I must ask him first.

He was very agreeable to the church taking an interest. No harm would come from it he thought and a visit from someone in the church would not arouse the mother's suspicions, as being part of the church's pastoral duty. He would be glad also for me to discuss this problem with anyone who I thought could help. I explained that it would be better for someone other than the school to become involved, someone who could keep a continuous watch on the situation. Would he leave it with me for the present? I would see him again when I had some information.

I thought first of talking to the minister, but fortunately I knew personally one of the senior laymen, a paternal and pleasant man. On the principle that it is better to talk with someone with whom one already has a relationship I outlined the case to him. He was helpful: the church had often wondered why the boy always departed at night often leaving things unfinished. No one had even enquired! However, he would call on the family, on the pretext of seeing the boy, and see how the mother was without arousing her feelings. He had not thought that the situation was this serious. He was a tactful man, and mentioned that they were very keen to enlist the boy's undoubted abilities to a greater extent in the church's activities. He came back to me later; the mother was greatly pleased by the interest shown, and by the interest in her son's services. Someone would call on her regularly.

When I saw the client for the third time, everything was fine. The interview lasted five minutes. Someone had been from church, ostensibly out of the blue. He could stay at church gatherings as late as he liked and indeed for other outings. His strain had gone. I never told him how it had been done, and he never came again, except to offer his thanks some time after he had left school and brought his fiancée with him.

Of course, this was an easy client to deal with in the sense that he was a gentleman, with a blameless school conduct record, and accepting him was an easy matter. As a counselling exercise it illustrates the following: I accepted his story as he told it, listening with concern, but without resentment even when he asked about my own family situation. Nothing was done without his consent. Had he not given me *carte blanche* I should have continued to meet him, if he had so desired, in the hope of sustaining him through a very trying home situation. I had some ideas of other agencies which could assist, but I refused to become emotionally involved in his home myself, or take over responsibility and action which were properly his. I limited the talks to matters of immediate relevance to his state, and did not begin to discuss, for example, the reasons for his mother's physical or mental condition, although this might have been necessary if no solution had been found, again to help him to understand the circumstances he had to face. None of my colleagues was implicated in this case. If I had made no progress I should have asked him if I could tell the headmaster and his form-master so that appropriate allowances might be made.

The earlier stages of this were non-directive: when the relationship was made we moved forward into action; he solved the problem really, by coming in the first place. My function was to provide the machinery – of which he was unaware.

CASE 3

Four very robust fourth-formers, aged nearly sixteen; tough by any standards, and generally regarded as potential trouble makers when they reached the fifth form: no polish at all, indeed rather uncouth and full of their rights: angry, verbose, slightly incoherent, with one exception. Work records variable, probably not up to potential in all cases. I had never taught any of them, but they had been in my house group for eighteen months, and had some vague pastoral responsibility for them. I used to meet them once a week in this capacity, in which they had always been ready to chat cheerfully about anything: admittedly most of this talk was complaint, but they were capable of serious discussion.

One spoke up like counsel for his client. They all played for the same school team, of which one of them was captain. He had been sent off the field for questioning a referee's decision. As was the school custom he was likely to be suspended: if this happened, they were all 'coming out in sympathy'. What did I intend to do about it? This was injustice and sorting this out was a housemaster's business – so I had told them. The victim was a fine player, an admirable captain who had been 'picked on' by a referee from elsewhere who was rather less than competent – to put it mildly.

Was this a storm in a teacup, just another piece of routine adolescent rebelliousness? I could tell them to be about their business and leave it at that: but they had challenged me on my own ground as it were. One cannot invite people to come with difficulties and then reject them.

They repeated the story, the principal in this episode contributing his version which was a verbatim facsimile of the spokesman's. Could I stop the suspension? After all, this kind of thing went on in industry and there was some current Press report of action by militant teachers which lent support to their request, of which they knew I was aware.

This was a matter of loyalty and injustice in their minds. For the moment I led them into a discussion about loyalty, my loyalty to my colleagues, too: the latter would be involved in any discussion about the suspension through a staff committee which dealt with such matters. After all it had not yet happened, and it might not happen. There was nothing to be done just then. Would they leave it with me to find out what had happened? After all, in justice they would not expect me, in view of what they had said, to act without hearing other opinions. The amateur lawyer nodded his head here and it looked as though his love of equity had overcome his passionate loyalty. I told them they were right to come, and undertook not to discuss this interview with anyone else. We parted on reasonably good terms.

In due course the staff committee met, and I made enquiries about the incident which had precipitated the interview. The offending player had, by all accounts from all sources, not been guilty of just this single offence. He was inclined to play robustly, even dangerously; in form and house games he was rough with smaller lighter younger boys, even when nothing was at stake: he resented criticism and was prone to muttering about referees, sometimes audibly; this crisis had been boiling up for some time. He was an exceptionally good player and the feeling was that if he could be purged of this lack of self-control he might seek representative honours. He was suspended for three matches, interviewed by the staff committee of which I was a member, and told clearly why he was being suspended.

The following day I met the quartet again. They were not happy. One of them said that the offender had been a bit of an idiot, and they were all in an upset, torn between their loyalty to their pal and the feeling that perhaps he deserved all he had got. The important thing for me was not to rub salt in anyone's wounds.

They talked a bit about the problem and I listened. Obviously I could now do nothing because I had accepted the verdict of my colleagues. One of the quartet was cross about this, but another asked me for my views about how and why the decision had been reached. I told them, and in fairness it seemed to coincide with what the offender had recounted after his interview with the committee. I ended by outlining the situation before them. Their pal was suspended; whether they thought this was fair or not was for them to judge, perhaps in the light of Press reports of dangerous play and misconduct towards referees in professional sport: if they decided to 'come out', people would respect some aspects of their loyalty, but against this others might think that they were simply supporting action which many people thought was wrong; moreover, not only would the school lose its best player, the rest of the team would lose their services also and might look upon this unkindly. They should go away and talk it out themselves: they could come and see me at any time. Once they had made up their minds they would have to abide by the decision and face it. I thanked them for coming.

The culprit saw his suspension out and continued to play afterwards. One of the others stayed out and never played again: the other two played in the culprit's absence. All four remained friends and used to chat with me as before. The one who came out in sympathy left school as soon as he could; the others entered the sixth form and became respected members of it in every sense. The culprit gained representative honours. All of them could have gone so easily completely 'off the rails' in the fourth form. Whether an hour or so in discussion of a matter of importance to them helped I simply do not know.

As before I listened and accepted them non-directively. There was already the seed of a relationship in my earlier informal contacts with them. My colleagues were involved, and there was a clash of loyalty on my part as well as theirs. The interesting feature is the identity between what the suspension committee said to the offender and what I said to the quartet. The offender did not accept it; the quartet did, at least in part. I attribute the difference to the fact that the quartet were treated as equals in their talks with me because I had accepted them first. The offender was treated as an inferior by authority. We were able to talk round an unacceptable position; he was not – he was given orders. I supported my colleagues' decision, despite the clients' protestations; for me the problem was not the decision, but how to interpret it to the clients in the hope that they would accept it. This case illustrates the use of counselling in many common school situations where matters which seem utterly trivial to members of the staff are immensely important to the youngsters involved. These boil up inside young minds and become potential and actual sources of real trouble and waste of talent – which were avoided in this case. I hasten to add that this was not the last occasion on which these young men needed help in making adjustments, but punitive action is not necessarily the best way of aiding this important process.

CASE 4

Sixth-former; gauche and nervous; absolutely trustworthy, courteous and very hardworking; entered sixth form with minimum 'O' levels and most selective schools would not have permitted him to go this far; great sense of responsibility and public service. I had taught him for four years, but not talked to him about anything other than my specialist subject, in which I knew his capabilities – and limitations!

He came with the *UCCA Handbook* and an army of university prospectuses. Which one should he enter?

The short and correct answer was 'None'. He had no chance of doing well enough to enter a university: he was already struggling with 'A' levels. The real problem was for him to accept this and look at something more appropriate. He was so set on his line of action, however, that I could not rebuff him directly. He had qualities which society needed. The puzzle was to find the means to use them, and face up to their suitability for him.

What was he going to do after university? He did not know. Why was he going to a university? A quite common tale emerged. All his pals were applying; his rather old parents were very proud of his progress so far; a university would cap it nicely; there were cousins, and assorted family friends and other relatives who had achieved university status; he must follow. We talked about this motivation for some time. He seemed glad to do so, although I had the feeling that we were not really making much progress.

He had great difficulty in marshalling his thoughts and I found myself becoming almost obsessed with the need to 'talk him out' of what seemed to me to be an ambition quite beyond him. This is a thoroughly unsatisfactory state of mind for a counsellor, and I began to seek ways of ending the interview, which had now lasted well over half an hour at the end of a more than usually exhausting day. I was rapidly running out of patience, clarity and understanding. I had to gain time without rejecting him.

I suggested that he go away and make a list of universities offering courses which suited him; he should also think about what he wanted to do in the future, whether he wanted to go into industry, some kind of social service, or an occupation which would marry his subject-interest with his undoubted capacity for handling young people; he had mentioned his interest in organisations like Cubs. Had he compared notes with his friends of similar ability? Did he think his parents were encouraging him in an ambition regardless of its suitability for him? This was as far as I felt I could go in dissuading him from a purely academic career in the next three years. Would he come again when he felt like it? He said yes.

I saw him as usual in teaching periods for the next month but he showed no inclination to talk again, and I thought I must have put him off for good, and that he was going on with his original ideas. Then he came again, with several offers from universities and allied institutions all with conditions almost certainly beyond his capabilities.

To my surprise he said he was inclined to accept the college with the lowest academic entry requirements; he had compared notes and work levels with his friends, most of whose plans were clearer than his own. His parents agreed with his decision: in fact they had largely left it to him, for, although they cared much for him, they had little idea of what it was all about, despite the academic attainments of some of his relations, whom he had in fact consulted, but who were all agreed that he must make up his own mind because situations had changed during the five or ten years since they had been educated. He was much more coherent on this second occasion and perhaps I was; certainly I felt better able to cope with him.

In the end this client entered a technical college because his results were inadequate for his earlier choice. This was the right result, in the opinion of those who knew him. He was not an academic, but a fine high-principled young man, with moral fibre and concern for other people, who was misled by intellectual pressure and status symbols.

There is nothing in this case of great counselling significance. I think he adjusted to his situation little by little; he never talked openly about parental disappointment; perhaps it did not exist. The important facet of it is the influence of the counsellor's frame of mind in handling a client. I stumbled clumsily through it. The client was very reluctant to take up other people's time; my view of his incoherence was dictated by my own weariness when he first called. His was a problem which would have waited a few days, or twenty-four hours, and I should have asked him to come at an appointed time. Some sixth-form teachers may think, in the light of their experience of this sort of guidance, that I have exaggerated the problem out of all proportion, that what he wanted was firm directive guidance and that I should have told him bluntly about his academic frailties which he must face. My view is that many sixth-formers are struggling to keep abreast of the standards demanded of them, and they are not helped by being told they are wasting their time. Indeed they have to look at themselves as this client began to do. There is always the hope that a process of self-adjustment may give them the confidence to do really well, and I have met several young men in this client's position who by being encouraged as well as helped to adjust to their weaknesses have risen to considerable academic heights. Personal development and maturity are often keys which unlock the door to unexpected intellectual ability. Nonetheless, this case displays the risks of becoming too 'counsellor-minded' and the need for teachers to be careful in making judgements about the most appropriate methods of handling clients in the light of all the information they have and provided the clients are in the frame of mind to accept guidance.

CASE 5 *

A physically robust character, noted as a bohemian or beatnik, in attitude and dress; intelligent and capable of good academic results at 'A' level; background unhelpful; a self-indulgent fellow, full of his rights and very alert to means of satisfying his material needs. I had never taught him, but had had occasional informal chats such as most masters have with sixth-formers. The visit was a complete surprise to me.

His opening remark was shattering: 'I think I am going nuts: you know your way around and I wondered if you knew a psycho chap who would see me!' To this I replied rather lamely perhaps, but with, I hope, the sort of sang-froid with which one greets the news that it is raining outside: 'Tell me about it.' It took him an hour.

The immediate occasion of his visit was a series of alternating depression and elation. Sometimes he felt depressed for several days, following this with a spell of euphoria of the same duration. At others the periods of one mood or the other were much shorter. What really bothered him was that these alternating cycles seemed to be shortening, each sometimes lasting only an hour or two before it reversed. He felt he had neither control over nor explanation for this phenomenon. He was frightened and indeed he looked it. I asked him to continue, despite his twice-repeated request for psychiatric help, for I did not think I had enough information at this stage, while he seemed to think that psychia-

* A shortened version of this appeared in an article in *New Society* on 23rd March 1967.

trists were sitting around waiting for clients. He went on. He
enjoyed his 'A' level studies, but did I not think that the whole
school was rather infantile? Without waiting for a reply he casti-
gated two of my colleagues by name for their complete inability
to make rational relationships with students of his age; they
treated him and his contemporaries as if they were first-formers,
and refused to discuss the quite fundamental ideas which inevitably arose during teaching periods. He and his fellows were idiots
by implication with no sense or individuality and no right to their
opinions. This was no way, he thought, to conduct what was in
effect adult education.

As I failed to react to this, except to invite him to talk further
about himself, he continued. He drank and smoked, and there
ought to be a smoking room in the school, but he never got
drunk. He spoke airily of his girl friends and thought precious
little of conventional sexual ethics, but the people of whom he
was really contemptuous were those who were trapped into 'shot-
gun weddings'; this was the essence of irresponsibility and
stupidity. He had tried pep pills, but becoming an addict was as
stupid as enforced marriage. I asked him about his home background. His parents were all right, as far as they went, which was
not very far. They did not oppose his continued full-time education, but his father thought that he could be earning a reasonable
living at his age; he also tolerated his son's social and political
ideas whereas the mother was appalled by them, although she,
somewhat passively, sympathised with his educational ambitions.
She had strong religious beliefs, which sometimes made life
difficult. He stopped for a few minutes and then asked about the
psychiatrist again.

'What about the family doctor?' I said. He began again. This
was no good. He did not want the family to be involved; they
knew nothing about the present troubles. He did not like the
family doctor anyway, but the crux was that this worthy would
involve the family and there would be an almighty fuss if his

parents were introduced into the problem. I told him that the family doctor or the education authority were the only straightforward agencies through which I could obtain the help he sought. He reacted vehemently; the second of these was worse than the first, for I must not mention this interview on any account to my superiors in school. He repeated yet again the request for psychiatry. Much of the earlier strain had by now disappeared, but he was still worried, and the alternatives offered had not helped him. I asked him to come and see me again, after undertaking to see whether anything could be done, and adding that he should not be optimistic about a successful outcome to my enquiries. This surprisingly cheered him up somewhat.

This case was potentially serious; all sorts of possibilities suggested themselves, including the thought that he had been less than honest about drugs and that he was on and off pep pills of some sort. I was very concerned about him, and his emphatic insistence on privacy did not allay my own anxieties. However, I thought I could probably cope with him, but like a client, I wanted to talk to someone about him. I could not consult any of my colleagues at any level, so I made an opportunity of discussing the case with a medical consultant whose judgement and experience with adolescents was known to me. The consultant, hearing the evidence presented by the client, said, 'I think he only wanted someone to talk to. If you are not happy when you see him again, let me know.' Thus fortified I awaited his return – a week later.

He came in most cheerfully. Without prompting he said that it had been nice to be able to blow his top. Since the first meeting his alternating moods had largely disappeared, he now thought he could sort himself out and the need for a psychiatrist had largely disappeared. 'Thank you for listening.'

From time to time thereafter we had brief chats round about the school, about social morality, drinking, smoking, usually when he was in a virtuous mood, but not always. This was not the last time that he was mixed up or angry with my colleagues, as his little confidences conveyed. In concrete end-product terms this case perhaps achieved little, and I look back upon it as a near classic case of non-directive counselling, depicting the more delicate professional problems with which a teacher-counsellor must be prepared to deal, and to face within himself before he becomes involved in counselling. I discuss these later; for the present they include:

1. Specific criticism of his colleagues;
2. Complaints about his superiors and the school régime;
3. The need for the counsellor to know where he can find advice to sustain him, or agencies which can act if necessary;
4. The absolute necessity for the counsellor not to be stampeded by his concern into premature or irrelevant action.

CASE 6

Four fourth-formers in a great state of agitation; of average ability as so far revealed; full of healthy mischief; having taught them myself for two years I was well aware of their efficiency at being thorns in someone's side; they were also capable of great helpfulness, reliability and charm.

Their tale was uttered amidst much interruption of one another in tones of outraged dignity imposed upon the stridency of partly broken voices. Its kernel was that one of them had been wrongly accused of a misdemeanour by a colleague of mine. The others had defended him, on their voluntary admission, rather rudely. Consequently they too had been threatened with castigation, whereas the real culprit, who had tried to own up and been suppressed by my colleague, had escaped retribution. This was not the offender's fault, and he did not know what to do, but had rather shirked coming to this interview. There was trouble in the whole form; my colleague was in for a bad time, the clients told me. Could I do anything? The master concerned was so cross that he would not listen to them.

There is nothing very unusual about this school situation, and one could easily dismiss it as another example of the kind of rough justice which is, inevitably perhaps, a part of living in a community. What use is there in arrogating it to a matter of principle? On the other hand these lads were really 'steamed up' about a matter of justice which was important to them. Moreover, I knew perfectly well, and they knew that I knew, that their form was a very tightly knit group who were perfectly capable of conducting a well-organised wrecking operation for the next two or three of my colleague's lessons. He would be badly harassed. if not resorting in the end to summary punishment by higher authority. Beyond this, a series of disrupted lessons is no use to anyone, least of all the boys themselves.

Would they leave it with me? Yes. They departed slightly mollified having unloaded their resentment.

I thought quickly. They and my colleague had to be put on speaking terms again with zero delay. It was a communication problem, exacerbated by combined bad temper. I called them back immediately.

'Would it be all right if I act as the middleman between you and Mr X?' 'Certainly,' they said. 'Will you do something for me then?' They agreed without questioning. 'You take this note to Mr X——' They cut me off with expostulations about the impossibility of approaching Mr X in his present mood. I said: 'Now look, all I want you to do is to take this note to Mr X and just say it is from me. You do not know what it is about. One of you can take it in, and wait for a reply. You will have to face him at some time, and if you do it quickly, resentment will die out. Otherwise it may take a long time to settle the problem. You asked me to help you. This is my suggestion. You do not have to accept it. I am not giving you orders.'

One said, 'I'll take it.' Off they went, not very happily.

The note stated briefly that I hoped Mr X would receive the bearer and listen to him, that they were very worried about the affair and were not sure how to put it right. I felt I knew my man better than they did, and the youths better than he.

All this had occurred during morning break time. I gulped a restoratory cup of tea and walked past the door of Mr X's room. He and the quartet, plus a fifth youth, presumably the original offender, were engaged in deep conversation. I met my colleague at the end of the next period. He was very happy, because he had been harassed, lost his temper and scarcely knew how to restore the position. Now, relations had been restored not only with the quartet, but with the whole form, and justice had been done. The boys too expressed their thanks later.

This apparently trivial little affair is more complex than it appears, for it embraces the relationships within the boys' group, their contacts with Mr X, his attitude to me, and mine to everyone else. The counsellor's job is to accept and work within this framework. It will be noted that I did not apportion blame, or accuse anyone of anything. This is no substitute for a solution, however temporarily satisfying it may be to the apportioner. It reminded me in some respects of those marriage counselling cases in which husband and wife are too emotionally involved to communicate, or have forgotten how to. Alas, not all cases are so simple or all teachers so co-operative. I ought to add that the boys were relieved too because Mr X displayed a sense of grace and justice. If we had not achieved what we appeared to achieve, I should simply have given them more time and opportunity to talk the problem out, but this would have been a harder task.

As a piece of counselling it was unusually short, and demonstrated how an adult's experience of handling people was used to correct the natural deficiencies in this respect of the young clients. In this respect it was directive, but giving names to actions is not a substitute for understanding what we were trying to accomplish – in this case an improvement in one small sector of personal relationships within the school – an enterprise which involved accepting virulent criticism of a colleague at the start.

CASE 7

Seventeen-year-old; quite bright; good potential, but showing signs of falling away; recently believed to have refused participation in school activities in which he excelled, letting other people down, on the grounds that he had 'dates'; suspected of being girl mad. I had only just started teaching him. The visit was not expected.

He was furious. In brief, his parents had been sent for, and he had been called in to the interview, during which he had been told that he had no chance whatever of going on to further education at eighteen plus, that his attitude was a disgrace and his work shocking; all this on the basis of information supplied by a colleague who did not know him, except as a name, only teaching him one period per week and never having talked to him. His father had thereupon laid the law down, withdrawn his promise to give the youth a moped, and waxed eloquent about girl friends and the general corruption of the client and his generation. Had I, who taught him, any complaint? Had I been consulted? Or the staff in my department? He had been deprived of something unjustly. He would not mind if the information had come from those who knew him, but this really was the end! He did not ask what I could do.

About fifteen minutes of concentrated spleen! He did not shout or rage. He was just angry. I agreed with him, as he told the tale. I was angry too for quite different reasons, but this was scarcely helpful to him.

I asked him what he was going to do about it. 'Nothing I can do really,' he said. 'You can't change my father's mind, only I can. But I had to talk to somebody and let them know what has happened. That's why I am here. I am going to show Mr Y (the provider of dubious or incomplete information) just what sort of a liar he is, if it is the last thing I do. I'm going to come back here one day, and say to him: "Do you remember saying that I was a disgrace and a slacker? This is what I am now. What have you to say?" Anyway, I am glad I have told you about this, because you ought to know.'

I said, 'You have answered your own questions really. It is up to you, and it is good not to have to lead someone round to this point of view. Let me know if you are in any further difficulty. By the way, how is the girl friend?'

He laughed, thank goodness. 'Fine; we just knock about together, and it is really rather pleasant. She even comes home with me – when my parents are in.'

The last remark was perhaps for my reassurance. All I did was listen to someone angry about injustice. He accepted it, as I did him. The remedy was in his own hands: nothing else for a counsellor to do except listen. This takes the strain out of many a difficult situation, or kills it in early stages.

Some teachers perhaps encounter many incidents like these during their careers. Do they understand what is entailed in dealing with them? Might it not be better to deal with them in traditional authoritarian ways? What sense or use is there in exalting them into 'counselling situations'? Are they trivial – to the clients? Are they within the province of a teacher's duties? Teachers must answer these and other questions for themselves, if they are really interested in counselling as an educational service for adolescents rather than a near-psychological gimmick. Do counsellors who are not teachers think that these cases come within the scope of counselling, or are they just first-aid operations of no deep significance? Do they understand the special problems which arise inside a school, and to which any counselling-teacher must adjust? Do we exaggerate the importance to adolescents of the relationships described in these cases? This last is difficult to answer, without the opinions of the clients concerned, and this I have not asked for. I would not suggest that the seven incidents were crucial turning points in the careers of the young men concerned, nor that these were the only occasions on which they needed further sustentation. However, I suggest that neither teachers who do not counsel nor counsellors who do not teach should underestimate the possible value to the clients of the attitude displayed by the counselling-teacher who may in fact be more sensitive to the totality of relationships within a school and more aware of the simple human needs of adolescent clients in our current social circumstances than people from outside the school.

These seven cases raise certain issues which in summary are these:

Cases 1, 2 and 5 raised potential, serious, social or domestic problems in all of which some knowledge of external supporting agencies was useful if not essential.

Cases 1 and possibly 5 involved matters of moral principle, especially Case 1.

Cases 3, 5, 6 and 7 involved my colleagues and/or the school régime.

Cases 3 and 6 were superficially common school situations which could easily have exploded into anger and rudeness and a final confrontation with authority accompanied by beating or detention.

Case 4 alone was a conventional scholastic-careers problem, but even this had external personal influences bearing on it.

Except in Case 6, where the colleague concerned had obviously to be aware of what had happened, no information was passed round the school by me; none was used on reports or any other formal documents. All the clients were 'steamed up' about something, and wanted someone to talk to, outside the family circle. They may be exceptional, although a long experience of adolescents does not lead me to believe that these were unusual youngsters as far as their general conduct and attitude were concerned. Whether they were representative or not, what influences urged them to seek the co-operation of a schoolmaster in matters which were extra-mural or partly so?

SUMMARY

Counselling is an experience through which one person, the counsellor, concerns himself with the life and affairs of another, the client, without becoming emotionally involved and seeking to impose his wishes upon the client. This demands that the counsellor accept the client and his situation as it is to start with, so that he can begin to help the client to find solutions to his own problems, and then prescribe them for him. Advice and guidance are not personal counselling, although the point may be reached at which these methods of helping people may become acceptable to the client as a result of a period of non-directive counselling. In practice, counselling in schools is a pragmatic experience, the counsellor adapting his approach, sensitivity and skill to the needs of the client, always remembering that he has experience to offer which an adolescent cannot possess.

Some aspects of counselling are illustrated by case-histories which exemplify the type of difficulty which a teacher-counsellor may encounter. There are significant differences between teaching and counselling, especially in the client's complete freedom to express himself uninhibitedly and the confidential nature of the relationship, the depth and duration of which may both be slight. There is need for knowledge of supporting agencies and for understanding the conflicts which may arise between the client-counsellor relationship and the more usual relationships within a school. Counselling is seen as a means of satisfying personal needs of a kind which the counsellor for all his skill, experience and sympathy may not fully comprehend. It is not a substitute for teaching, but a supporting service; it may turn out to be a replacement for formal punishment methods, or for preventing situations in which these might be thought appropriate. Neither is it a once-and-for-all solution of any one client's difficulties, because these alter rapidly in adolescents, but the relationship itself may prove enduring and therapeutic, even in retrospect on the client's part, for it is the relationship based upon acceptance of the client as he displays himself which gives counselling its unique value.

II. Why Personal Counselling?

The word 'counselling' is applied in a restricted sense to the art and skill of professional psychiatrists, psychotherapists, and clinical psychologists as well as to the methods used by some categories of social case-workers. All of these are highly trained specialists, with professional qualifications in their field. Yet the National Marriage Guidance Council uses the word to describe the work of its carefully selected and trained volunteers to whom those in marriage difficulties can turn for help in solving their own problems, and who do so much admirable work with adolescents in schools and clubs. For some time American schools and colleges have had specially trained teachers on their staffs, or non-teaching adults attached to them, called counsellors, whose function is to provide a personal guidance service outside and different from the academic teaching given by the usual staff. Furthermore, counselling is now being advocated for prisoners and Borstal inmates, some local authorities have established youth counselling services staffed by professional or voluntary social workers, a few others have appointed counsellors in schools. Nowadays therefore the word counselling is used in contexts far removed from clinics of highly trained analysts; 'counsellors' includes a larger number of less highly trained people no longer primarily devoted to the affairs of the mentally disturbed, but concerned instead with the activities of a wider spectrum of humanity, the majority of whom could be described in everyday terms as quite normal. To such people the situations which formed the themes of Chapter I might not be surprising because they demand on the teacher-counsellor's part an attitude common to all counsellors which distinguishes them from, for example, the former, traditional sources of advice outside the family: doctors, lawyers and clergymen. The authority of these professions was based upon greater knowledge and higher education than that of their patients, clients and parishioners. Consequently they tended to give advice, direction and instructions based upon that authority. In contrast, counsellors do not give advice, provide instruction or exert authority. In treating the mentally ill, for example, the analyst depends greatly on the degree of co-operation he can elicit from his patients even when he may have to prescribe certain forms of treatment, for the success of this may itself be limited by the quality of the relationship between analyst and patient. To these categories of workers, professional or voluntary, the teacher-counsellor in school must belong. He too must accept his clients as he finds them. These other counsellors listen to their clients and prompt them to find their own answers to their problems, using the counsellor's skill, insight and understanding to pilot them through their difficulties: their relationships are all based upon partnership, not authority, and through them the client can be helped to come to terms with himself, or be cured of his affliction with the co-operative assistance of whatever clinical services and methods may be available. All this the counsellor in school must do also. Yet it is evident that the relationship postulated for the counsellor and his client stands in marked contrast with the traditional student-teacher relationship so familiar to everyone. Why then is attention given to counselling in schools? In my view, this is partly because attitudes in schools are changing of themselves, partly because changes in family and church influence compel schools to examine their internal relationships, partly because adult society is itself disturbed by what it believes to be adolescent assertiveness and self-isolation, and partly because some adolescents seek it.

THE INTELLECTUAL BIAS OF SCHOOL ACTIVITIES

It is not surprising that society should look to the schools for remedies for adolescent turmoil, whether the latter is exaggerated or not. For everyone goes to school for at least ten years. No other social agency or public service has such a potentially significant opportunity of moulding the minds and characters of its clientèle outside home. And if the latter's function and nature is evolving, as some sociologists claim, then school influence may be enhanced by default, as it were, of family influence. The main function of schools has until now been intellectual, in the sense of being directed towards mental training and learning, with smaller contributions from physical and craft training to buttress the central goal. Perhaps unfortunately, the term 'intellectual' is now applied to that sort of education which prepares students for university and other forms of further education. Yet basic Arithmetic and English for the fifteen-year-old school leaver are intellectual activities for him, as much as Further Mathematics and English Literature are for the potential university entrant. The level appropriate to a particular school or student does not affect the fundamental nature of the process, or the consequences which over-emphasis on purely intellectual activities can produce in the students concerned. An educational process which is largely intellectual is limited and narrow, because it tends to neglect other facets of a person's total being, such as his stability, courage, determination, adaptability, altruism, and other attributes which determine his social conduct and attitudes. These of course lack the objectively measurable or examinable properties which make intellectual education easier to assess and therefore perhaps more attractive; and such personal qualities, on the face of things, do not seem to be relevant to success measured in intellectual terms. Moreover intellectual failure has tended to be regarded as total failure, and it has been my frequent experience to help students at ages eleven, sixteen and eighteen, who have been 'written off' solely because they failed to reach a particular level of intellectual attainment by a certain age. In such cases helping means mitigating the sense of social rejection which this failure had brought in its train. Fortunately, there are abundant signs that schools no longer universally reject students on the restricted evidence of intellectual performance. On the other hand, they are less knowledgeable about how to offset intellectual inadequacy. They may be certain that they have to help students to come to terms with their own abilities and deficiencies in school subjects and to accept the probability that what they might like to do may in fact be beyond their capabilities in the world as it is; that they must help them to utilise fully the qualities of mind and character which they possess instead of feeling rejected and unwanted, and to understand that inability to achieve ambitions does not make any person less valuable, good or helpful. But schools are less certain of how to carry out this often extremely difficult process, and a wide variety of pastoral care services are scarcely more than a tentative probing towards solutions of the problem. There is something more in this personal education than good careers guidance, however valuable this is, something less businesslike and tidy than advice, something which has more personal meaning to the student. Counselling can contribute to this 'something more'. It does not replace or conflict with intellectual and other school activities; it works alongside them and makes them understandable to the student. It may well involve those who counsel in problems like the first case in Chapter I, because situations of this kind are part and parcel of the whole person who is the client, although they may not be immediately evident. There is considerable evidence to show that this process is needed for students of high intellectual calibre too, for they display signs of rejection and inadequacy not because they are intellectual failures but perhaps because their narrow education has totally neglected other facets of their whole being and rendered them incapable of coping with real life. Schools are in an admirable position to assist in correcting such maladjustments, or prevent their emergence, provided that at least some of their staffs are capable of the adjustments which a counselling service demands. Yet – why put yet another burden upon the schools? Why not the Church? Why not the home?

DECLINE IN CHURCH INFLUENCE

Churches seem no longer to command the attention of more than a minute fraction of the population between thirteen and twenty. Even children of devout and liberal church adherents desert the cloisters which their parents regard so highly. Why this is so is beyond the scope of this book. Churches keep the interest of a larger proportion of children aged twelve or under, but there are few clergymen or committed laymen of any Christian communion who do not ask – and who can answer the question – 'How can we keep the teenagers?' I believe that this rejection of the Church is a loss, not so much of habitual adherence, the value of which may be doubtful, but of contact with some principles of social conduct and of the opportunity to think about values and about people other than one's self. It is probably true that adolescents do not reject religion itself, but the absence of any acquaintance with the institutions and communities of religion – the churches – seems to create gaps in human relationships and ignorance of ethical principles which compel adolescents to mature in isolation from influences which have materially affected our social evolution, however much they may be criticised. Moreover, this deficiency has contributed to a sense of 'not belonging', an unhappy and intangible feeling which some churches have shown themselves able to correct. What little experience there is of personal counselling in schools suggests that it could partly replace this function of the Church.

CHANGES IN FAMILY INFLUENCE

The earlier suggestion that the nature of the family is changing arises from the observation that parents seem now to be more content to leave their children to the care of people and agencies outside the family than they used to be. Children are sent to

Sunday School, but the parents do not attend church themselves, and are angered when, in adolescent years, their children refuse to attend any more and quote parental disinterest as support for their own abstention. Parents are glad that their children attend Scouts, Boys' Brigades, Girl Guides, Youth Clubs and other organisations, but show little interest in what their children do when they attend. Moreover, they are reluctant to offer help in running or supporting them. Parents' Associations attached to schools are often fortunate to command the active attention on serious, as distinct from social, occasions of half their potential membership. Some will not take the trouble to consult with teachers even at times convenient to themselves. My own enquiries over a period of years suggest that only one adolescent in twenty discusses any serious problem with his parents. Some parents are not interested; they will not offer time and patience. Others are admitted by their children to be incapable of giving the help and guidance that the children need; they are in this context inadequate people. The ethics of this shift of emphasis from the family to other agencies are not the issue here: the issue is that many youngsters have to make decisions unaided by parents, even about their own careers and futures. Deprivation nowadays is expressible in terms more of lack of interest, communication and affection than of inadequate food, clothing and accommodation. Adolescents are driven to talk among themselves as a discrete community within the larger community. For all their knowledge and sophistication this is often a case of the blind leading the blind. Sometimes they talk with a selected teacher, who may find himself involved by parental default in the total personal life of the person who comes to him. This is the beginning of counselling. The involvement, as the illustrative cases show, can be very deep. It seems, in some cases, to compensate for the deficiencies caused by changes in family relationships, and it seems probable that schools may be compelled to undertake this service much more extensively, by making counsellors available to provide the personal relationship which statutory or voluntary agencies cannot or do not supply, however admirable their material aid.

TELEVISION

Connected with changes in the family is the complaint that television is to blame for much adolescent aberration. Television brings into the home vivid presentation of social and moral issues in real and fictional situations. Little harm, and much good, would accrue if parents were prepared to discuss these matters with their children, but many have neither the wish nor the ability to do so, and children are left to come to their own conclusions, without benefit of conversation with anyone other than their own generation. And yet, the Granada TV series on 'Understanding', in which adolescents talked with adults as equals, showed that such conversations can be rewarding to both generations. It also enabled many teachers to make more relaxed personal relationships with their students, and involved the schools in matters which some people think ought to be talked out at home, matters which imply a serious rethinking of the relationship between teacher, home and student, and can lead the teacher into the position of a counsellor.

IMPENDING RISE IN SCHOOL LEAVING AGE

Raising the school leaving age to sixteen also challenges the relevance of traditionally authoritarian student-teacher relationships. Experience with the growing number who stay voluntarily to that age will be valuable, but these are volunteers, and many teachers look bleakly upon the prospect of controlling an army of educational conscripts despite the long-range social virtues of the change. Their sixteen-year-old charges will virtually be young men and women, demanding treatment as partners rather than children to be ordered about. Certainly much serious thought and planning is being devoted by local authorities to make this extra year useful and rewarding to the students. Team-teaching, activity-spaces, modern approaches to religious education, the enlightened use of literature, community service, home management and careful vocational guidance are all discussed sensibly. But these are largely techniques and the extent to which they succeed in the students' minds will depend on the personal relationship between them and their teachers, and the extent to which the latter can accept them as individuals in co-operation. Some teachers will find this difficult; others will adapt well. To the latter, and especially those who can accept their students to the extent illustrated in the cases cited earlier, may well fall the heavy burden of sorting out problems of relationships with their colleagues and the students. A counselling service for sixteen-year-olds may become prescriptive as one means to achieve this harmonisation in the first few years after the leaving age is raised, particularly to help the sixteen-year-olds to adjust to a new situation which they may resent. Certainly traditional forms of punishment will achieve nothing but resentment if attempts are made to use them to correct maladjusted relationships, a form of school malfunction which really requires correction through the kind of relationship which exists between a counsellor and his client.

INCREASING USE OF IMPERSONAL TEACHING AIDS

Educationalists of every kind foresee the extended use of teaching aids, electro-mechanical, optical and electronic devices, the function of which is to increase teaching efficiency. Much instruction in knowledge and skill can be more effectively imparted by films, film-strips, closed circuit television, teaching machines working to instructional programmes and other machinery than by traditional 'chalk and talk' methods. Society has a duty to see that educational resources, especially those of scarce man-power, are most effectively deployed. On the other hand, much 'blackboard' and other orthodox teaching is successful because it involves the personal relationship between teacher and taught; and it is a common experience, not to be lightly discarded, that the popularity and success of certain subjects in a given school are due to the personalities of the individual teachers concerned, rather than their expertise in a specialised subject. The influence of such teachers extends beyond the confines of their own specialist rooms and subjects, and often ensures that their schools are harmonious as well as stimulating places with a good 'atmosphere'. For students need people. Perhaps it is a rather conservative view, but I recoil from the prospect of an automated programmed-learning factory, bereft of personal relationships and influences, masquerading as a school. This could give us the worst effects of that concentration upon purely academic learning of which I have already written, without any of its compensation. To offset the depersonalisation which increasing gadgetry can bring, schools will need teachers who are able to make the kind of relationships with their pupils which counsellors employ for therapeutic purposes, teachers who can impart a sense of personal value to students often working in an impersonal situation. One can thus foresee two classes of teacher at the extremes of a whole spectrum of pedagogic ability: those who are effective organisers of hardware, deploying it in the interests of lucid instruction, and those whose interest lies in satisfying the personal needs of their students. The latter group will help students to develop their whole being, and in some cases at least this process demands counselling in the personal sense with individuals or with small groups. To do this requires certain appropriate qualities, just as the users of gadgets must possess organising and planning capability. Both types of teacher are needed; between the two there will lie a range of teachers with mixed abilities, and there will always be that small minority who can meet the demands of every situation, organisational or personal, those who are the first-class managers, the harmonisers of community relationships and inanimate equipment.

ADOLESCENTS SEEK COUNSELLING

The last and perhaps most important reason for the existence of a

personal counselling service in schools is that some students appear
to need one. In the tradition of counselling, all the young people
who have come to me to talk about personal problems, which are
apparently distinct from the customary interest of a school, have
come of their own volition. Their enquiries have not been
solicited. In retrospect it probably began with some enquiries
conducted in the course of writing a degree thesis, which invited
pupils in a secondary modern school to express their opinions and
attitudes about certain topics in the curriculum. The roles of
teacher and student in this enterprise were reversed; they were the
givers and I the receiver of information and opinions. A sense of
partnership grew, and was extended to informal meetings with
individuals and small groups at lunchtime. The initial interest in
the purpose of the enquiries gradually spread into wider fields of
personal relationships, home problems, attitudes to parents and
girl friends. The crucial factor was surely the complete privacy
with which their opinions were treated. Even then, seventeen
years ago, there was a readiness, if not a need, to talk with a
teacher in quite informal terms. The word 'counselling' at that
time was scarcely in the educational vocabulary. Later, working
as an educational counsellor for the Marriage Guidance Council,
I met some of my school pupils in the wholly different circumstances of youth clubs to which I had been invited, where there
was no discipline in the school sense and any relationship which
there was between the counsellors and the clientèle was based on
partnership, not authority. These pupils carried the club relationship into the school, and I was approached by some of them with
personal problems, in confidence. Others collected in groups to
enquire at first into my motives and attitudes in doing this work.
Subsequent experience of marriage counselling with young
married couples has given further evidence of the need for some
kind of private personal guidance service and not restricted to
purely sexual advice. More recent experience of late teenagers in
court has suggested that some of them might never have appeared

there, if at some earlier stage they had had someone to whom they could talk and who could have helped them to understand themselves and their situations.

I do not doubt that other teachers have had similar experiences, with different origins, for different reasons, and in different contexts. Such teachers have with their students that 'quality of relationship' which I mentioned earlier. They are poised to look at counselling as a purposeful school activity, as an aid to the total educational process in their own schools. They are an integral part of the educational establishment, having a relationship of some depth to start with. They are in a position to accept the burdens which changes in social habit, alterations in teaching method, and the expressed needs of their students put upon them. We must now study the problems which stem from this involvement.

SUMMARY

Counselling is now used in wider contexts than those of the clinical consultant, but all counselling demands a degree of co-operation between client and counsellor which is distinguishable from the usual authoritarian relationship between pupil and teacher. Yet this new duty is put upon schools in the interests of their pupils, despite their earlier preoccupation with purely intellectual achievement, which has tended to cause total rejection of some of their pupils. This, counselling can mitigate. School counselling could also offset in certain undefined respects the declining influence of the Church; it might compensate for apparent changes in the structure and significance of the family and the effect which the intrusion of television may have had upon social value judgements. Impending changes in education, particularly the wider use of semi-automated teaching aids and raising the school leaving age, call for careful thought about the meaning of personal relationships in school. Above all, some students think that a counselling service is necessary.

III. Problems and Possible Solutions

Some of the doubts and uncertainties which some people associate with counselling can be partly dispelled by discussing illustrative cases and looking at the general principles which can be derived from them. On the other hand the cases may themselves raise new doubts and thus leave us with an even longer list of dilemmas and difficulties which must be resolved before teacher-counselling becomes acceptable in principle let alone a practical proposition. Some of these are administrative or organisational, and perhaps an inevitable consequence of the novelty and unfamiliarity of counselling at this stage. I deal with these in Chapter IV, but, as counselling becomes an educational custom, an accepted feature of the school scene, they may be expected to disappear. Other difficulties are, however, more fundamental and have their origins in the dual role which a teacher-counsellor has to play. I hope to show later that the ability to accept this duality on the teacher-counsellor's part, and on the part of others involved in the educational process, in fact contains the solution to many of them. But if we define the duality more precisely and effectively it amounts to this: that when he counsels a teacher-counsellor has a duty to his client solely and exclusively, a duty which the illustrative cases suggest is different in kind from his second and more conventional one. The latter is the formal duty to his school and to the community of which the school is a part, the general nature of which is understood by that community and forms the basis of the contract of service between him and his employers. This, it is scarcely necessary to discuss here. At a first glance it might appear that this division of duty is quite artificial. After all, a teacher, his school and the community are presumably partners in a common enterprise — that of prospering the total personal development of the students who are the counsellor's clients: there is thus a communion of interest which is above details of school method, approach or internal organisation. Nonetheless, the harsh realities of day-to-day school life when studied in conjunction with some or all of the cases cited in Chapter I may induce in teachers' minds not only doubts about the procedures and relationships of counselling, but also conflicts of interest and attitude. And these conflicts or dilemmas may not exist only in the minds of teachers who counsel: they may equally concern committee-men, parents and others concerned with education. These conflicts or dilemmas are expressible in the convenient form of the questions which follow below, questions to which teacher-counsellors, as well as those who employ or work with them, must be able to supply answers if they are to go about their counselling without apprehensive glances over their shoulders. A furtive atmosphere, fraught with suspicion of any kind or from any source, is not conducive to good counselling and does not help the client. The list of questions is not necessarily exhaustive but it includes those which, in my view, present teachers with the greatest difficulty:

1. Has a teacher a duty, as an agent of the society which employs him, to put across to his pupils what we might call an 'establishment' or accepted view in matters of social conduct?

2. How are relations with his colleagues affected by the apparently very permissive view he takes of, and the highly confidential relationship he has with, his student clients, whom his colleagues also teach? More practically, how far should he accept and justify criticism of his colleagues and the régime of his school?

3. To what extent can a counsellor who teaches keep his interviews confidential, and why ought he to do so?

4. Does not the special nature of the counselling relationship expose him to abuse by those of his clients who might seize a

golden opportunity to exploit the unusual situation?

5. What are the effects of the counselling relationship upon formal work and discipline in his school?

6. Despite the tentative official support for, and concurrence in, the use of counselling as an educational service, what view do parents and authorities take of it and its implications?

I attempt in succeeding pages to analyse these questions and to present tentative answers. The doubts I express are not only my own as a teacher looking into the counselling relationships which I have experienced, but also, I hope fairly, those of highly competent and thoroughly human teachers, who have no counselling experience, whose ideas expressed in conversation I value highly. These doubts exist. They must be countered; resolution of them has to be sought and in terms which are acceptable to those who hold them. The order of treatment is not necessarily one of importance. Each question is as significant as the others. The division between them is in parts quite arbitrary because one facet of the counsellor's skill in practice and art in relationship is inevitably and inextricably bound up with the others. The separation is inescapable, however, if any analysis of these questions is to be attempted.

1. THE TEACHER'S DUTY AS AN AGENT OF HIS SOCIETY

Teachers are concerned about this, not only because of their own positions and because they often feel that the young people in their charge need handling in different ways from those which are customary, but also because the adult world outside still expects teachers to inculcate a basis of social and moral conduct into their students as a matter of duty and contract; perhaps with moderation and reason, probably with some tolerance of disagreement and not necessarily with the threat of sanctions. Many teachers accept this, and are often concerned at the conflict between what society expects them to inculcate and what society itself exemplifies. When an outbreak of adolescent aberration occurs, the frequent cry is: 'What are the schools doing about it?' 'It' includes drug-taking, vandalism, sexual misconduct, theft and the rest. Some teachers who take seriously the duty implicit in these questions and who are also deeply interested in counselling or EPR will perhaps be disturbed by, for example, the situation presented in Case I, which is a useful one to discuss in this context, although it is in my experience exceptional in its complication and seriousness. Some of them would contend that for a counsellor to accept the suggestion that a seventeen-year-old boy and a girl should live together amounts to complicity in and condonation of a legal or moral offence, and that even an expression of disapproval would, of itself, be insufficient action. If a teacher, who is an agent of national and local authority, who stands on occasion *in loco parentis* and who by statute has children in his care for long periods, does not condemn this suggestion, who will? I do not want, in parenthesis, to obscure this issue by debating the ethical basis of such a condemnation – to do so is outside the province of this book. Simply for convenience, I assume that this basis is sound. I have great sympathy for those who see this as a real dilemma and the ends of counselling are not served by denying that it exists in the minds of many teachers whose approach to their work is humane and kindly. It is a dilemma experienced less by professional analysts, marriage counsellors and others who do not live with the duality of the teacher's duty. To resolve it we have to go back to the beginning, at the risk of some repetition.

A counsellor cannot help or serve his client in any way unless he accepts him and the client's view of his own situation as a starting point. The client can only start on the journey towards what I call recovery, in whatever sense seems appropriate to him, from where he is. The old tale about the man who asked a passer-by how he should get from where he was to another place has some relevance here; for the passer-by, it is alleged, told his enquirer that he would be wiser to start from somewhere else.

A counsellor must not, metaphorically speaking, tell his client to start from any other place than where he is. Of course, a counsellor, for a variety of reasons, may not like what the client tells him, and it may be revealed as the interviews progress that the client's original story was an inaccurate account of his state of affairs. Neither of these circumstances, however, relieves a counsellor of the duty to start with the client's inaugural account of what he believes the state of his affairs is. A counsellor who cannot accept this is really asking his client to start with what he, the counsellor, would prefer to hear. The client is thus placed in the position of having to meet the counsellor's needs, a position which is a reversal of the proper roles of client and counsellor. In this reversal of roles the counsellor in effect encourages his client to deceive himself, to pretend, simply to please the counsellor, that the situation he wants to talk about is something other than what it is or what he believes it to be: he is not aiding his client to begin the difficult task of looking at his situation sensibly, of taking appropriate action to adjust it or coming to terms with it. He is abetting his client in blinding himself to the facts of his situation, real or imagined. This is especially reprehensible when dealing with adolescents who are ready enough to indulge in escapist self-deception without encouragement from adults. Thus, a counsellor who rejects by open disbelief or moral condemnation what his client has told him brings about a deterioration in the client's state as measured in the counsellor's own moral terms, of which truth is a part. Such a counsellor, by rejecting at the outset what his client believes to be the truth about his circumstances, achieves the very opposite of what he seeks to accomplish in counselling.

It is true that teachers are under constant social pressure to correct what is conventionally called 'wrong behaviour'. Whether condign punishment in the form of pedagogic retribution is as all-powerful as some people imagine is beside the point. The relevant issue is that this social pressure overlooks the need to investigate the causes of adolescent misconduct, and we can only ascertain this by unearthing as much truth about an adolescent client's condition as is humanly possible. Then we are able to look for sensible solutions to the problems which lie behind the errors – if such they are. The whole process can only be started at the position in which the client is, or believes himself to be. If we examine Case 1 in these terms, taking his problem as he presented it revealed the state of relationships between the respective parents and the young people in the case. Counselling elicited the possibility that the genesis of the course of action advocated by my client was the rejection of both him and his girl friend by their parents, who exacerbated the original problem by a refusal to face their own responsibilities, by rejecting the two younger people and their ambitions instead of talking about them. Had the parents sought advice, affectionately and sensibly, they might have reached a happy solution of the problem and restoration of relations with their children, instead of 'sweeping it under the carpet' by pretending it did not exist and threatening to expel them from home. They failed in their parental duties just as the youngsters at first refused to look at the possible consequences of their proposal. By any standards, counselling or otherwise, this at least offers the young client grounds for a plea of mitigating circumstances, but no counsellor can offer mitigating circumstances for pretending that what he does not approve of has no existence. His task is to deal with what exists, namely the client's situation and circumstances, not to turn his back on it.

At first I considered the possibility that the client in Case 1 made his suggestion in order to shock me. I do not know what ultimately happened to him and his girl friend, apart from their further educational careers, but he adhered throughout the series of interviews to his suggestion with quite unshakable consistency. It was therefore reasonable to believe that it was a genuine one – a conclusion I reached very early in the counselling. Directing the client's attention to what was entailed in their proposal offered a better route to more sensible, or more moral – in some people's view – solutions than outright condemnation; and not only this, it was a more compassionate treatment of the client as another human being who was in trouble. Continued rejection scarcely constitutes the most merciful way of dealing with those whose recent lives have been a series of rejections.

Let us now look at this dilemma in another way. The client and his girl friend turned to one another because they had been cast out by the very people whose duty it was to sustain them in their educational ambitions – their parents. Why the parents did this, I do not know; there were certainly no financial reasons, but it was clear that at no time had they taken any interest at school in their children's prospects. However, more mature adults might still say, despite their sympathy, but in the light of their knowledge of the world, that the relationship which grew from this meeting of lonely people was at least more likely to be transitory than permanent. But to the parties concerned it was at the time immensely significant and it may possibly have diverted them from other potentially more dangerous and unfortunate actions, indulgence in alcohol, drugs, or suicide; admittedly there was no evidence of any proclivity to these, but the possibility was there. The relationship conferred a degree of stability and responsibility upon the client and his girl, perhaps not in orthodox terms, but certainly real enough. It is possible that it might give both of them the resilience and strength to provide society with two more educated people, instead of two more castaways. Of course, much of this is surmise, but it provided good cause for not saying to them: 'I reject your analysis of your difficulties and your solution to them and with them I reject you, because I am a teacher and an agent of society which disapproves of your views; you may do whatever else you like, as long as I do not know about that of which I do not approve, because I am a teacher.' It seems more sensible to display human sympathy and compassion with the situation, to work with whatever qualities of loyalty and responsibility are exhibited in the client's exposition of his case in order to examine more clearly than he can – for he is emotionally involved – the possible consequences of his actions. Moreover, it seems to me that the attention being given to the possibilities of counselling in schools is an admission by authority that counsellors exist to accept situations as serious as this one, if need be, and to hold out a hand to those who are in such depressing circumstances. If this is not part of their purpose, school counsellors are superfluous.

Again, consider a client who comes to a counsellor because he either wants confirmation that his proposed line of action is appropriate or is uncertain and wants help. In the first case he probably needs the benefit which everyone derives from talking with a good friend. On the other hand, he may need some serious advice about appropriate action in the cricumstances he has described to the counsellor. In the first case he is set upon a course of his own choosing, from which he will not be diverted by outright condemnation; in the second he is seeking possible alternatives. The client in Case 1 was in both these categories, for he had a solution in mind, and was also seeking information. If I had adopted a rigid moral position by condemning out of hand what he suggested he would have retired from the dialogues, if experience is any guide at all, and the possibility of discussing other courses would have disappeared. He would have been more likely, in the remote possibility of his staying despite my rejection, to react against what he thought to be my prejudice by clinging more firmly to his own ideas. He might well have gone further, to the view that because he found no understanding of his attitude in me, he would also meet rejection everywhere else, that there was no use discussing it at all, that all adults were as disinterested in his difficulties as his parents were at an earlier stage in his life. This scarcely seems to be a rational solution to a social problem. Far better, therefore, it is for the counsellor to maintain contact by accepting what the client says and then encouraging him to think about a course of action which general human experience predicts is more likely to be disastrous than not, giving him information which helps him to ponder. This simply means that counselling only helps a client when the counsellor forgets his own attitude to the client's views and thinks more about why the client turned to him.

The teacher's position as an agent of society certainly makes us think about his moral position, but a direct attempt by a counsellor to inculcate moral values is less efficacious than the indirect importance to the client of the relationship of mutual confidence which counselling enables him to make with an adult. The personal role of the counsellor here is more significant to the client than professional, factual or moral guidance. In the long run his personal role may achieve what we can describe as moral transformations or the selection of the most appropriate future, assuming that these are thought to be desirable consequences of counselling, but these are not the personal counsellor's central purpose. The teacher who can accept his clients, but who is nonetheless deeply concerned about what in very general terms we may call his position as a moral agent of society, should not be unduly apprehensive about the possible long-range moral depreciation in his clients which he might think would follow from his acceptance in confidence of suggestions which seem to him to be wrong. The fact that he can listen makes it possible for his client to consider ideas which he had, up to the point of counselling, either not thought about at all or previously rejected. Moreover, at this point it is important to remember that counselling discussions are always conducted in total privacy, and apart from the client and counsellor no one knows that they have taken place. This distinguishes the counselling situation very sharply from discussing theoretically a question of principle in public, or indeed in a classroom, divorced from the facts of a specific situation such as that outlined in Case 1. Isolating theoretical problems of social morality from the client's total personal environment creates an artificial situation, which it is not the counsellor's function to analyse. He is concerned with actual people, their situations as a whole and with making relationships which they believe to be valuable and sustaining. It is not for him to judge, even if he is capable of doing so, whether the relationship and the series of discussions have been sustaining or helpful to the client. There is no end product to the process such as marks and orders of merit to which teachers are accustomed, and by which they estimate the success or otherwise of their work. Because many teachers cannot escape from the urge to achieve an apparently concrete result they find counselling situations exasperating. They may correct poor performance in formal work by changing their methods or increasing the pressure on pupils because they have traditional means of determining success or failure by grades, marks and ranking orders. Poor marks may be a guide in instruction but there is no progress report in counselling other than a counsellor's self-criticism and analysis, for only the client can say whether two or three counselling sessions have been therapeutic in any way. Counsellors have to live with this uncertainty and not expect the righting of wrongs, overt moral transformations, or increases in self-control. These they may seek within themselves, especially when they are confronted with cases their natural reaction to which is 'I must do something', but they cannot act upon these private self-indulgent wishes without destroying the relationship between them and their clients.

2. THE EFFECTS OF COUNSELLING UPON RELATIONS WITH COLLEAGUES

Criticism of colleagues and superiors can be at least embarrassing. Moreover, occupational loyalties of every kind are frequently thought to be at least as important as a sense of service and duty. Teachers are not exempt from this loyalty and will defend colleagues whose attitudes and motives are questioned by those outside the profession. Yet, in the intimate private relationship between client and counsellor, the latter can be concerned only about the prospects for healthy growth and maturity of the clients, about the problems which they present and in which they need help. They are the only people who matter; the counsellor's position is subordinate to that of the client. Counselling is ill-suited to those who see it as an avenue for personal advancement for this puts the client's interests second. We shall see later that counselling can bring general benefit to a school atmosphere, but professional loyalty and ambition have no part in this, and clients' criticism of colleagues and superiors must be put in its perspective as a normal hazard of the service.

Much adolescent criticism of the adult world is intended to shock or test a counsellor's reactions. The situation is confidential, there are no sanctions; it seems a golden opportunity for the client to say what he wants without fear of reprisal. This is a safety valve, and if a counsellor accepts it without demur, as if it was only to be expected as a normal reaction in the circumstances, the criticism exhausts itself. Young prisoners would comment abusively about police, probation officers, magistrates and prison staff, as a prelude to discussing quite seriously the role these people have to play in society, given a quiet acceptance of their expostulations. Adolescents in youth clubs attack vehemently their parents, police, clergymen and teachers. As soon as they see that the counsellor is not disturbed by this, but accepts it with interest, their fury subsides. A cool question, such as 'Why do you feel so strongly about this?', is then a stimulating beginning of that self-exploration which is central to counselling. The client who is confronted with this question has to start looking at himself instead of indulging in slanging matches with someone from another generation. This takes time and patience; it requires help from the counsellor in framing his questions and comments, but always the criticism is the starting point. This is simply a particular case of the principle of starting with the client as he is, of accepting him and his situation and feelings and exploring what lies behind them. For much aggressive grumbling and complaint is rooted in unhappiness, frustration and ignorance, including ignorance of the developmental changes in the process of growth which create these aggressive ideas. An explanation of this can be helpful. But, granted acceptance, and quiet explanation, there often remains a residue of criticism which is not rooted in emotion but is rational and thoughtful.

Two aspects of this are important. The first can be quite briefly dismissed. If counselling is being considered, as it is, at a high level, as an educational service, it seems a fair assumption that criticism of the educational system, in principle or in detail, is regarded as an acceptable part of it. Criticism of colleagues and immediate superiors has to be accepted by those who counsel and by those who employ counsellors and work with them. Clearly much will depend here on how counselling is introduced to a school. The second is less easy to dismiss because it entails consideration of the unique position of the teacher as a figure of authority, and the consequent sensitivity to any form of challenge in the sense that it undermines, or appears to undermine, the teacher-counsellor's own authority. If a student criticises one colleague there is every likelihood that he will criticise another. It is thus conceivable that his client will criticise him to his colleagues. What therefore is at stake in coping with this is any teacher-counsellor's view of himself. Sensitivity to criticism of others in private reflects uncertainty about his own position vis-à-vis his students, and his motives in teaching. Four of the seven cases quoted in Chapter I include critical comment about my own colleagues. This can be accepted if one accepts that a client who criticises Mr X to Mr Y will possibly criticise Mr Y to Mr Z. Criticism of one's colleagues implies criticism of one's self, and the issue at stake is acceptability of censure of one's self, when that censure is given privately, and one is in fact unsure whether it has been given or not because it is concealed in criticism of a colleague. It is not so much criticism as the uncertainty which worries many of us. If it does concern a teacher that one of his students may comment adversely about him to a colleague, then the counselling situation is not for him. I look upon criticism of me, given in the special conditions of the counselling process, as a means of improving the relationships between me and the students with whom this improvement is needed. Teachers can improve the image of any of their colleagues in the eyes of their students by using the counselling situation: but public debate in class is a less suitable means to this end. On occasion students have asked me to advise them in counselling on improving their relations with colleagues, using the counselling relationships as a bridge towards better contact with others. This is a rather rare sign of maturity, but it illustrates the possibilities which counselling offers for improving the atmosphere in a school. It also demands that one's colleagues should understand the counselling approach and be assured that it is not being exploited to their disadvantage along the lines suggested in subsequent pages. One would not expect such maturity in the majority of students under the age of seventeen, especially in an educational system in which private personal counselling is still something of a curiosity. In essence those who counsel need to look upon remarks about their colleagues as a start towards better relations within the school and should not react defensibly and angrily because they see criticism as objectionable in itself.

Criticism in these terms can be a useful beginning for the discussion of loyalty with a client. Adolescents understand the meaning of this word within their own groups, and they react favourably to the idea that this is found elsewhere. Even if one cannot resolve criticism usefully in the ways suggested, adolescents are often surprised to find that adults can accept it, and this is a salutary experience for those whose experiences of adult reactions to criticism elsewhere have been confined to 'shut up' or a cuff about the head. Youngsters' criticism is often a safety valve for their own pent-up feelings, and screwing this down is not a sensible safety precaution. For an adult to accept it as a rational kindly human being, not necessarily agreeing with the justice of it but recognising the client's right to make it, often soothes the arrogance or anger of a client, and enables the counsellor to start to find out what the real trouble is. It also alters the authoritarian image of the teacher-counsellor in the client's eyes. Teachers should not be over-concerned with the problem of professional loyalty provided that counselling privacy is recognised. At this point a great burden is put upon a teacher-counsellor, because his motives and good faith are at risk in the eyes of his colleagues, who may not accept his position as easily as he can. His colleagues must recognise what he is doing and accept that he may receive comments about them. He must not use what he hears in the counselling room for any purpose other than to help the client. Good faith and professional dignity are destroyed by mentioning to one's superiors or other colleagues that 'X' in form five has made some nasty comments about Mr A. This jeopardises Mr A's position and may be based on remarks out of context; even if he does not mention the source of his information, which would endanger the client too, the counsellor is here denigrating Mr A and improving his own position by using confidences which X has given him. It is a different matter entirely if X agrees that the counsellor should have a private word with Mr A to improve relations with him as Case 6 exemplifies. Here, no one else knew of the approaches of the clients to me or of me to my colleague. The machinery of the school was improved by a discreet consultation. However, it is in the possible exploitation of counselling interviews by counsellors for their own ends that the greatest dangers of professional criticism lie. The only safeguard against such abuse of the counsellor's position lies in his proven personal integrity, and the recognition by his colleagues that he is the right sort of person to do this kind of work. Clearly this has connections with the problem of selection and training of counsellors and the way in which their work is introduced into the general organisation of the school. This introduction must be accomplished by those responsible in such a way as to achieve maximum confidence in them and their work.

3. STRESSES CAUSED BY THE PRIVACY OF COUNSELLING

Teachers are trained or conditioned to remembering data, marks, opinions and attitudes. They record them by habit and use this information to compile reports and in interviews with parents. Much of this is confidential in the sense that it is intended for use by school and parent only. But the counselling situation is totally different. What transpires in the counselling room is private to counsellor and client, unless the latter agrees that it should be communicated to someone else who can help if necessary, in the opinion of the counsellor. We have already dealt with criticism of a counsellor's colleagues as one breach of trust, and adolescents are equally sensitive to breach of confidence. The common difficulty is the teacher's obligation so to recondition himself that if he counsels he does not disclose anything that is said to him during counselling, regardless of pressures driving him to do so. It is not easy, for example, to hear colleagues discussing a student's performance and attitude, in total ignorance of the problems which he has revealed to a counsellor and which have a bearing on his school performance. There is a great temptation to correct what is overheard in this way by revealing what the student has said privately. Such revelation might conceivably prove to be in the student's interest in the long run but the breach of faith is more damaging. If the counsellor feels that he ought to advise his colleagues the proper approach is to explain to the student why he feels his confidences or relevant parts of them should be quietly mentioned to certain colleagues. If the student does not agree, however, the counsellor must keep it to himself until the time comes when he does. There is an interesting parallel here with the attitudes of parents, who sometimes give to a school information which they think would help the school to understand some of their children's attitudes and reactions which might otherwise seem inexplicable. Quite frequently parents, while confiding in the Head of the school, ask that the information should go no further, because they think it would be better if the children concerned were left to work out their own salvation without being thought of as special or abnormal cases. They give the information to Heads for guidance in case difficulties should occur. If they do, the Head can then, and only then, advise the staff concerned. Similar feelings seem sometimes to be in the minds of those clients who insist that a counsellor must not, under any circumstances, divulge anything to his colleagues or superiors. Often this turns out to be the right course, largely because having talked to the counsellor about the problem, a client feels better able to live and cope with it by himself. Where this is not effective, and the client seems to be stumbling from one difficulty to another with the counsellor's colleagues, the counsellor can then see his client again and say: 'It would be better if you would allow me to mention what you have said in confidence to the Head or Mr X. They too would then understand the problems which make life difficult for you outside school, and it would be easier for you to end this endless series of confrontations with my colleagues which seem to be causing so much friction. Better still – you could talk to them yourself, and I can prepare the way for you with them, if you like.' This approach very rarely fails, especially after two or three counselling interviews in which the *bona fides* of the counsellor have been established beyond doubt. It is possible that some clients delay agreement to breaking confidence solely to assure themselves of a counsellor's good faith. Once this good faith has cemented the relationship, the counsellor's advice is acceptable. The rider to this is that, if the client persistently refuses consent, the counsellor must resist any temptation, in the staff-room or elsewhere, to pass on what the client has told him.

The seal of confidence puts strains upon a counsellor in other ways. Suppose the client describes in a first interview what seems to be a very serious situation; drug-taking and sexual deviations at home are two examples of information given to counsellors which come into this category. What is the counsellor to do? There is a temptation immediately to inform relevant people and agencies in a perfectly sincere attempt to put right that which is obviously wrong. Yet the real priority is to establish that the client is telling the truth. Many adolescents are emotional, and eager to bolster their egos by imaginative tales, and counsellors need to be extraordinarily careful that they do not take precipitate action upon any information, for this may turn out to be fictional. Sometimes, too, hair-raising tales are recounted to test the reactions of the counsellor, as with staff-criticism. If a counsellor acts emotionally or precipitately on startling information, and involves third parties in what ultimately proves to be merely a display of imagination or bravado, he can not only destroy the relationship between him and his client, but he may also cause serious upset in a family, in which relations were good, by his failure to realise that this display of highly coloured fiction was but a short-lived stage of emotional development. The state might well have passed almost unnoticed if the counsellor had done nothing but listen and the child concerned have moved on into healthy development, a development distorted out of all proportion by the consequences of the counsellor's emotional over-emphasis and well-intended but hasty action.

The counsellor can only establish the truth of what his client tells him by further interview, yet, if the client does not want this, the counsellor can do nothing. If further interviews take place, and it seems that what he hears is true, his first duty is still to re-member his seal of confidence. For it is in this understanding that the client has divulged the serious facts he is considering. His sec-ond is to say to the client: 'I cannot help you unless you agree that I consult someone else.' That someone else may be the Head, an appropriate colleague, the police, the local children's department, or any other suitable agency. Here it is advantageous if there is more than one counsellor in a school: few situations are more helpful than that of having another counsellor with whom to consult before referring cases of this type elsewhere, when the client has agreed. If the client does not agree, a counsellor has no right to do anything, however much he feels that he should take some action, either as an ordinary person or as a teacher who believes he has a duty to society. If inaction troubles him, he can assuage his conscience in three ways: if he had not been a counsellor working under specifically private conditions, the information would never have come to his notice; he can still sustain the client in times of stress by talking the matter over, because the client finds the relationship helpful; the client may finally agree to outside help being invoked or reach the point at which he can act himself. For a counsellor to act as the agent of any other social organisation without the client's co-operation is totally to destroy his image as a trusted confidant and friend. Because this is his image he can encourage adolescent clients to help themselves, by turning, with his aid and, when appropriate, to those specialist agencies which are more competent in their fields than the counsellor is by himself.

Teachers in girls' schools will, doubtless, raise the special problem of the pregnant pupil. Surely, they urge, if a student seeks a private interview during the course of which she says that she is pregnant, the teacher concerned must tell someone. The girl must certainly tell someone and counselling in this situation should be concerned with discussing whom should be told, who can help her most in her difficult situation. Do her parents know? Does the putative father know, and what does he think ought to be done? Do his parents know? Does she herself know who can help her before, during and after the birth? Does she wish to keep or adopt the child away? Has she seen her doctor? In fact, is she certain of her condition? Does she wish to continue her education, and if so, does she know what arrangements can be made for her to do so? Counselling here is intended to give the girl the resources to solve

G

her own problems by seeking the guidance of those agencies and people who are best equipped to help, who are specialists in the appropriate services. She may indeed ask the teacher to help her by getting in touch with some of these, or to meet the parents with her and help her to tell them. If this is so, it must be done; but it is in every sense better for the girl to face her own family on her own, fortified by the resources she derives by communicating confidentially with someone else, in this case the teacher-counsellor. Teachers here are sometimes more concerned about their own position than the girl's. When a girl tells her parents about the pregnancy and mentions to them that she has informed her teacher, there is always the possibility that they may turn up at school in anger because the school did not pass the information to them. The answer to this is quite plain: 'Your daughter gave me this information in strict confidence as a friend, and I could not break that confidence. Would you break a confidence?' There is no need to add that the girl's reluctance to inform her parents first is possibly a sad reflection upon the relationship between them and her, as the fact that she is pregnant may also be. When such furious parents have calmed down, through the therapy of an interview with the girl's counsellor, it will then be worth discussing the family relationships and where the parents may have gone wrong. Although blame, if that is the word, is not necessarily wholly attributable to parents, they too so often need guidance and help in their share of the solution to the girl's problems. It cannot be over-emphasised that, in dealing with emotional vicissitudes like this, the primary problem is the girl's; the status of parents and teacher-counsellors is a secondary matter. At worst any solution may be making the best of a bad job; at best it is to see that the wisest possible decisions are made in the interests of the girl and her impending child. High-flown moral and professional attitudes are not useful contributors to these ends, and the counsellor's function is simply that of the trusted adult to whom one can talk in confidence and who will hold out the hand of support to a youngster who has landed herself in a situation for which she is at least partly responsible, and in which she feels utterly lost and betrayed. Although it is obviously a problem in which girls' schools more often have to supply help and consolation, young men sometimes come and admit that they are responsible for their girl friend's pregnancy, feel that they have a responsibility to carry, and seek help in undertaking this responsibility. They need the same confidential and understanding treatment as the girls. Apportioning blame is no use to either sex: most of them in such predicaments are worried enough without coals of condemnation being heaped on the fire of misery. The counsellor's business is to help them to face the facts of the situation and decide what is to be done, not to display moral outrage which other pepole will do far more effectively than he.

The fewer people who know about students' problems which are as serious as this the better for everyone concerned, students, parents and school alike. There is no room in counselling, therefore, for the person who rushes gleefully into the staff-room with the news that Jean in lower fifth is pregnant or Smith in lower sixth takes drugs, that Robinson in 5A has got his girl friend into trouble, or Susan in upper fourth is the tart of the local coffee bar. There are people who revel in this squalid gossip-mongering, and regrettably there are some of them in schools. One of the interesting experiences of Marriage Guidance Counsellors who are invited into schools to conduct group discussions on personal relationships in privacy is that they are sometimes questioned by members of the staff afterwards. Not all of this questioning is directed to facts about method and results: some certainly is intended to find out who said what in these discussions and these counsellors deliberately refuse under any circumstances to identify members of their groups, even under what amounts on occasion to cross-examination afterwards by some members of the staff, who, despite a high degree of professional competence in teaching their subjects, seem at times to enjoy unearthing evidence of what they think is the depravity of their students. The glare of publicity can only be damaging to anyone who is in real difficulty, and for whom the dependable understanding of a counsellor in quiet privacy is the nearest approach to solace, apart from a guide to practical and acceptable help, which the unhappy client so desperately needs.

When all is said and done, everything depends upon the school atmosphere and the view of counselling which is taken by Heads of schools, local authorities, boards of governors and parents. We shall discuss this in a later section of this chapter, but it seems mandatory that a counsellor can only work to the point of helpful involvement in so serious a problem as a pupil's pregnancy if the ground has already been prepared among these extraneous people so that they trust the counsellor's confidential work and attitude implicitly, and look upon him or her as a necessary aid in the whole business of helping young people to manage their affairs, even if they are not affairs in which the adults themselves would care to be involved.

The business of writing traditional school reports is sometimes imagined to be a potential source of difficulty for a teacher who counsels, because he must, in effect, divide his knowledge of students into two parts: that about which he can write in conventional reports, and that which he must not mention because it is the product of confidential counselling. This does not seem to me to be a real obstacle to the dual role. A teacher's remarks on a report are based upon accumulated records, marks in examinations and impressions of class work in comparison with other members of the same group: his information is detailed, often based upon long-term observation, and is as objective as he tries to make it. By comparison, his counselling records, as we shall realise later, are very brief and necessary only to record what has gone before, the gleanings from private interviews, and intended to help in making a significant relationship with his clients. The methods and aims of the two sets of data are therefore quite different, as are the circumstances under which they are compiled. There should therefore be little difficulty in separating the two categories of information. When a teacher-counsellor comes to write formal reports about students to whom he has also been a counsellor he may indeed write them with greater care and under-standing because he has some insight into the whole background of these students and understanding of the kind of guidance they need in a school report. He must not disclose in a school report, which is a document about work, effort and progress, anything which comes to his notice about the personal life of a student as a result of counselling. Neither is there any need for, or duty upon, him to do so, for contacts with parents in counselling matters should be conducted not through formal reports but via more relaxed private personal meetings when they are needed. Behind this difficulty of reports, however, lies the character and capability of the individual teacher, who, if he cannot divide his functions in this particular way, should not counsel.

4. EXPLOITATION OF COUNSELLING BY UNSCRUPULOUS CLIENTS

'Don't they ever call you names?' This apparently trivial little question was once put to me, presumably in the belief that a youngster who meets a counsellor in total privacy will grasp eagerly a rare riskless opportunity to tell this adult exactly what he thinks of him in forceful, if not lurid, language. I suppose this is, on reflection, a possible occupational hazard of counselling, although I have never experienced it, and if a counsellor agrees to meet a client who knows that the interview is going to be confidential then he must be prepared to accept everything that comes his way in whatever terms the client wants to use, four- and five-letter words included. It is beside the point to argue that abusive outbursts undermine a teacher's authority and insult his professional status, for the arguer fails to appreciate the distinc-tion between the relative publicity of the class-room and the privacy of the counsellor's office in which neither authority nor status has any relevance. I recall once being told in quite extravagant language by a couple of burly fifteen-year-olds in a secondary modern school to mind my own business when I reprimanded them privately for some minor school offence. This was long before I had heard of, or started, counselling, but my rather surprising reaction on this occasion was: 'That's a silly thing to say.' The offenders blushed, appeared to be somewhat shaken and retired in partial disorder. We got on very well together from that moment onwards. The point of this anecdote is that I was not disturbed by their crude verbiage and showed them that I did not think it was important. What teachers do if this happens in a class-room is another matter altogether, not for discussion in these pages, but a counsellor's reaction in this eventuality is to say: 'Why do you feel so strongly as to use this kind of language?' 'Does it help?' 'Why?' 'Are you used to this kind of language?' No counsellor has anything to fear from accepting a client's abusiveness, for it is a symptom of the client's insecurity, frustration, anger, or background custom, a fact of his total situation. Simple questions, like those suggested, make the client begin to think about his own behaviour, knowing that his counsellor is not to be shaken out of his calmness, and that he himself will not be rejected by the trivia of habitual or angry bad language. For a counsellor to regard the latter as a personal affront indicates only that he should not be counselling, because he sets his own view of his prestige above the need to learn all he can about the client and his conditions.

The episode quoted above is in my school experience unique, and whether counselling individually, or in clubs or with prison groups, I have rarely had bad language used. Moreover, to my knowledge, no one had ever boasted to his friends that private consultations were an excellent opportunity to express one's opinion of a schoolteacher without fear of reprisal. It is perhaps true that there is a very small minority of adolescents who might be tempted to exploit the counselling situation in this rather odd and pointless manner. But who loses anything in any respect by this? Certainly not the counsellor, for he has made himself available to help or listen to clients who are in trouble. That the latter have initially responded in an abusive way tells us something about them, and in the long run they can always remember that, as no consequences have ensued, they can go back to him and use his services more sensibly. And one final thought comes to mind; a considerable effort on the part of an intending client is needed before he approaches his counsellor for the first time: he has to summon all his nervous resources. It therefore seems unlikely that many prospective clients will exhaust their resources simply to indulge a childish – not an adolescent – or a petty spite impulse. In the end, however, teachers who contemplate counselling must be prepared for even this, and if they cannot bring themselves to face it with unruffled demeanours they should not counsel.

5. EFFECTS OF COUNSELLING UPON FORMAL WORK AND DISCIPLINE

If we believe that it is a school's function in modern times to develop all the potentialities of its students, then, notwithstanding the doubt which has been cast in earlier pages upon the value of undue emphasis on academic performance, regardless of level or measuring technique, a duty still lies with schools to enhance the intellectual development of students as far as their capabilities allow. Doubters may comment that it is all very well to have counsellors, but hours of counselling are not a substitute for hard disciplined work, for external examinations or not. This is partly true, but it mistakenly regards counselling as a substitute for rather than an aid to work; for counselling aims *inter alia* at discovering why a student is not progressing in his formal work. Once this has been decided, and counselling is quite often the only way of doing so, then measures which are appropriate to the individual student can be taken to improve his performance.

Students whose work is defective can change attitudes as a result of counselling, and their work often improves. In parenthesis, this is a point at which the benefits of the teacher-counsellor are best experienced. He can see the significance of both the counselling and formal study, whereas the 'pure' counsellor could find himself holding an opinion which is diametrically opposed to a specialist subject teacher, and appearing to take a view which is as one-sided as that of a subject specialist of the client's position in school, that he thinks formal study is relatively unimportant because he is not involved in it and does not have any responsibility for it. Yet we have seen already that a counsellor can act as a bridge between his colleagues and their students, and that this might become a significant function of a school counsellor. The fact that he teaches also makes it easier for him to understand the attitudes of his specialist subject colleagues and translate these attitudes to his clients. He is aware of their difficulties as well as those of his clients; this strengthens the influence he may have upon them, and makes him a much more effective partner in their total education.

Here it may be argued that any teacher worthy of his calling does his best in his subject periods and outside them to find the reasons for a student's bad performance. Often these reasons may be obvious, but unhappily too many teachers fall short of the best in their calling in this respect and reject students simply because they, the teachers, do not or cannot probe deeply enough into their students' attitudes and motives, or attempt to cross the barriers of personal animosity which at times prevent a student from giving his best. For success in formal teaching is as often a function of the personal relationship between teacher and taught as it is of instructional competence or student interest in a subject. Counselling can be instrumental in improving this facet of the educational scene. I remember at this point a husband whose marriage I had been counselling for some months. He and his wife were emotionally involved in the difference which arose between them; they were unable to look at their relationship in a sensible manner, and fundamental courtesies had ceased to exist between them. I, the counsellor, stood outside the emotional situation and was able to bridge the gap between them, until they had reached the point at which they could understand their own and each other's attitudes much more clearly. They were then able to re-establish their earlier happy relationship. Although parallels like this are not wholly valid, I think a teacher-counsellor can take up a similar position in a confrontation between a colleague and a student about whose work the colleague complains. He stands outside, is not personally involved in it, but can see the attitudes of both clearly and so help to resolve the differences. A further common feature is that, as with the marriage to which I referred wherein both husband and wife sincerely wanted to improve their relationship when they first came for counselling, a prerequisite of successful counselling between a colleague and a student is that both have a will to improve relations between them. Failure is very likely if either colleague or client refuses to budge from his existing attitudes. My experience is that this is rare, but there are teachers who feel so personally insulted by a student's incapacity in their subject that they almost refuse to admit his existence as a person in any circumstances. When this happens the counsellor can only help the student to live with his colleague's antagonism, to survive and progress despite it.

Counselling is almost certain to be ineffective unless the counsellor is prepared for the client who looks upon counselling time as an escape from the realities of lessons with a teacher he does not like. After discussing his client's attitudes, he must begin to turn his client's attention to the facts of this situation. If he does not, he is encouraging the client to escape from reality. The time must come when he has to say that there is no more he can do: for, in the end, the client has to come to some sort of working relationship with the particular teacher. He has to go back to him; he cannot escape for ever into the imagined seclusion of the counselling room. The point at which the counsellor suggests that meetings with him must end is a matter for him to decide, perhaps in consultation with the teacher concerned, and the only proviso is that the door must be left open for the client to return. No one can say that so many hours of counselling are equal to so much frustrating teaching, but I suggest later that a real value may accrue from withdrawing a student from lessons in a subject in which he is not working, counselling him during those periods and then allowing him to return.

So far in this section we have considered the relationship between counselling and formal work, which to many people is the main function of a school's existence, and how counselling might in principle be used to improve student performance. There are also connections between counselling and the problem of discipline, student control or school harmony, whichever we think is the most appropriate term to use. There is a real fear in the minds of some teachers that counselling, and indeed other pupil-centred activities, are synonymous with, or likely to lead to, school anarchy and chaos. Those who hold this view are apprehensive that if we devote too much time, and in the extreme case any time, to the personal needs, wishes or whims of students, we may totally undermine the coherence of school communities, reducing them to disorderly pandemonium, in which everyone does what he likes, when he likes, where he likes and how he likes. My own philosophy of education is largely pupil-centred: but I do not believe either that young people should be encouraged in the notion that what they want when they want it is what they should do or have, or that counselling is directed to gratifying these wishes. The examples I have quoted earlier may have indicated clearly enough that this totally self-indulgent attitude is not intended to be encouraged by a personal counselling service. Nonetheless, the feeling persists in some teachers' minds. Although I suspect it to represent simply that fear of the new and unknown which is common enough in conservative minds – and teachers tend to be a conservative body – we have to reckon with it, because it is one of the facts about the environment in which counselling occurs. To disregard it, to sweep it away as if it were of no consequence, does not solve a counsellor's or a teacher's problems. These are real enough, and scarcely dissipated by some rather confused thinking about child-centred education, much of which originates in the minds of educational theorists far removed from the practical and worrying exigencies of the class-room. For there are class-rooms, especially in the tougher areas of our larger towns and cities, in which fear, confusion and violence are real enough, and the counsellor's approach seems at first irrelevant or irresponsible. Yet, if it is not simply another facet of the total free activity school of thought, how is it related to, or useful in, solving the problems of day-to-day school discipline, or harmony as I prefer to call it?

At this stage we remind ourselves again that the teacher-counsellor's unique advantage is that he does both jobs, teaching and counselling, in the same school; he is familiar with the problems of the teacher who is in difficulty with one group of students or another; he knows what he himself seeks to achieve through his counselling. The dual role makes it feasible for him to attempt to bridge the gap between his teaching colleagues who are having a difficult time in exercising class-room control and the students who are ostensibly the cause of it. He can counsel in conduct problems, as he can in work problems: the two may often be closely related. But counselling in both contexts raises similar difficulties, and I return to one which I touched upon when dealing with school work, the implied abandonment of the voluntary principle in student counselling, for hitherto I have considered counselling as a voluntary act on a student's part. This is easier for students of sixteen or more than it is for younger ones, and there may be good grounds for directing students to counselling. It is difficult for some of them to take the initial step of calling on the counsellor, whom they have hitherto seen only as a teacher; but there seems no reason at all why a student should not be instructed to come to a counsellor and invited to express his feelings in private. The initiative comes from the counsellor, if necessary, through his colleagues; the student does not have to summon the resources to take it. It may take rather longer for the counsellor to break down the student's feelings of doubt about the relationship than if the student had come himself, but this directed counselling eliminates the delay caused by the client spending time summoning the resources to see the counsellor or to realise his need to do so, if indeed he ever reaches either point of decision. There is a risk, of course, that teaching colleagues might be tempted to send for counselling every student with whom they have the slightest disciplinary difficulty. This, I believe, is likely to be greater when the counsellor is a non-teaching specialist rather than a teacher-counsellor: the former could easily become a sort of educational dust-bin into which the teaching staff would discharge every piece of student iniquity. Whether this would be so or not, directed counselling is more likely to be effective when it begins after close consultation between a teacher-counsellor and the colleague who has troubles, because the former would have a clearer idea of his colleague's particular problems as well as the view he takes of the student concerned.

Counsellors who find themselves implicated in relations between staff and students, wherever the initiative started, need to be aware of the possibility that some sorts of anti-social behaviour may be the outcome not of bad relationships between teacher and taught, domestic stress or out-of-school social background influences, but of illness or mental disorder in varying degrees. Diagnosis of the latter is not a matter for amateurs, and it must be re-emphasised that counsellors are not psychiatrists and should never be tempted to pretend they are. On the other hand, such phenomena as explosively violent temper, unusually savage attacks on others, continuous decline in attainment and complete lack of any emotional response to any situation *may* indicate a seriously disturbed state in the client, which only specialist advice can investigate and confirm or deny. Counsellors engaged especially in staff-initiated counselling have to know where they can find such advice for referral. Discussing such cases with other counsellors is also extremely helpful. These are exceptional cases, and opinions about the value of counselling should not be governed by them or any other relatively rare occurrences.

Because they teach, teacher-counsellors have to exert formal discipline in the normal course of their work, and students may find it confusing to accept him in a dual role: they may find it difficult to judge which of the two roles he is playing at a given time. The essence of the counsellor's position here is that he is known to be fair-minded and considerate because of the attempts he has made to establish a relationship with the offender. Punishment, if he has to use it, is therefore generally accepted without rancour because it is known that the counsellor's analysis of the events leading to it is thorough and free from emotional prejudice. Although teacher-counsellors hold a special position in their schools they have in general terms to subscribe to whatever set of rules apply to the school community because they are a part of it. Situations do occur in which counselling fails to elicit from certain students any degree of co-operation with or understanding of the needs of their fellows, as distinct from the purely arbitrary rules of the establishment. I discussed this with a group of seventeen-year-old sixth-form students after some fifth-formers had been punished for persistent and inconsiderate disturbance of their schoolmates. This group felt that there was a limit to which a counsellor can go in school, and that, in the last resort, after repeated attempts in the counselling room to evoke co-operation and self-analysis, when a student persistently disturbs his colleagues by his conduct – and this was the critical factor in the group's view – then the school must do what the larger community outside has to do: it must apply sanctions and express its disapproval, even if this entails rejection of the offender and the apparent departure of the counsellor from his principles.

Three of the group to whom I posed this problem had some benefit from counselling in their earlier years, but felt strongly that one might spend days trying to communicate with offenders of the type we were discussing and yet fail because they would not co-operate. Time spent so profligately on a small minority whose only identity lay in near lawless groups outside the school could be better employed on others who would appreciate and respond to counselling, but who would be neglected by the counsellor's exclusive preoccupation with unusually anti-social cliques. Moreover, the group felt that resentment could be aroused among the more co-operative students by over-concern for those whom they regarded as layabouts. Society always contained an unco-operative element, and, they felt, was entitled to reject it and bring retribution on it, if necessary.

These opinions from young men who had at one time been on the borderline of anti-social behaviour are stimulating and perhaps startling in their orthodoxy. They highlight the counsellor's dilemma between his counselling and enforcement roles, and admit that he cannot always avoid it. They also contradict the idea that counselling, if it is adequate, eliminates the need for punishment. If it fails within the context of the school, more specialised outside guidance may be indicated, a possibility which did not come within the purview of the group's analysis. They also neglected the salient facts of their own cases, namely that they had sought guidance at an earlier age, and that the offenders in the given instance had not sought the benefit of the counselling which had been helpful to themselves. Perhaps the frailties of the offenders we were discussing should have been noticed earlier: events might have turned out better if this had been the case so that they were directed to counselling, and specialist treatment sought if this was thought to be necessary. This is my own opinion, for many students prefer to have 'six of the best', get it over with and pay a penalty so that they feel justified in repeating the offence, rather than face their own immaturity and inadequacy, at least at the beginning of counselling. In the long run, however, coming to an understanding of themselves, by talking their problems out, is a more searching and therapeutic experience than punitive action. The optimum age for attempting this varies with the student, but the period from fourteen to sixteen years of age, the time of emotional disturbance, may not be early to avoid later trouble.

If, however, we direct students to counselling, or a teacher attempts to counsel those he actually teaches, demands on counsellors' patience and self-control increase markedly. Students whom I describe as 'directed clients' might be expected to show sullen resentment and resistance to invitations to talk, to be more frightened of incriminating themselves than students who have come for counselling of their own volition, and less ready to accept the teacher's confidential counselling role. Counsellors must be prepared for long periods of silence, for refusal to answer questions, for furtive escapist glances out of the window, and the inability to look them straight in the eye. They will sometimes encounter flat unemotional responses to any kind of suggestion, non-committal evasiveness of every issue, and an apparent lack of loyalty to anything, only profound self-pity, excuses and indulgence. The first comments made by these directed clients are likely to be evasive platitudes, of the 'I was not doing anything' type, when they are not being accused, uttered in toneless voices and intended to make a counsellor react with traditional pedagogic outbursts of anger. Failure to achieve this outcome produces only further silence. The overall picture of the client here resembles 'dumb insolence'; yet behind every such case, however uncooperative the client's demeanour, there lies some personal story, some explanation of the client's history, or the unique chemistry of his character. The problem for the teacher-counsellor here, as the senior students' group suggested, is whether he has the time or the skill to deal with such psychologically difficult cases. If he has not made a start after two or three periods of counselling, he must be prepared to face possible rejection by the client and pass him on to specialist service. This is better counselling in the school situation than frustrated persistence and misuse of time valuable to others.

Even a counsellor's skill and care may prove abortive in the face of overwhelming odds represented by bad home conditions, by environmental influences which make a complete nonsense of almost any attempt to discuss in the simplest terms ideas of social conduct in which other people's rather than the client's wishes are respected.

Individual counselling on its own may be less effective here than the kind of group discussion therapy in which I have participated, with others, with young men under twenty-one, serving prison sentences of three months or more, who had been, with rare exceptions, through every sort of corrective or penal process available before they finally finished up in gaol. The method used was simple: a pair of counsellors met about ten prisoners in a closed room, without any supervision by the prison staff. We, the counsellors, were received with a mixture of hostility, cynicism, and curiosity, which generally persisted in about a quarter of the clients throughout the series of four two-hour sessions held at weekly intervals. The reaction of some of them to a relaxed, unofficial and spontaneous approach was in the end, however, almost pathetically appreciative: they ultimately began to look at themselves and the society which rejected them with slightly less jaundiced eyes. For most of them this appeared to be the first occasion on which they had made a relationship, however fleeting, with anyone older than themselves which was not one of conflict and antagonism. Other attempts have been made on similar lines, but using police and magistrates among others as partners in discussing the problems which confront society and the criminal.

I am not suggesting that counselling or discursive methods which are being tried as means to rehabilitating those who have already fallen foul of the law are necessarily appropriate to schools which have difficult anti-social groups with whom to cope, but the following experience is interesting. In attempts to solve student-recalcitrance by counselling methods, I have observed one interesting reaction which appears to contradict the hostile reactions described earlier. This was that certain fourth- and fifth-formers who were sent for arrived expecting a form of retribution, but were so relieved to find that this was not the case that they talked with the utmost frankness about the difficulties they were experiencing. I am not attempting to elicit general rules here: clearly the two opposing opinions which have been stated about the possible benefits of what we may call staff-initiated counselling make a generalisation impossible. There is, however, some substance in the general thesis that if the adults of this world hold out their hands to the young they will find that they are grasped willingly in the majority of cases. Counselling in school is fundamentally this, and a development of it could mean a great step forward in the development of staff-student relations.

There is a more practical side to this. Most teachers will recognise the group of three or four fifteen-year-olds whose future prospects are difficult to assess, whose work is variable, who rarely exert themselves, but who are supremely skilled and subtle in the fine arts of class disturbance. I call them the hecklers. They give one or two of their teachers a really unpleasant time: they pick their men with remarkable insight, and reduce their classes to virtual chaos. The staff concerned may have some responsibility for this, but this is not the issue at this stage. What remedy is there? Cane them? They have had this so often that they cannot count the occasions. Keep them in after school? This happens so regularly that they regard the extra time in school as part of their timetable. Give them impositions? They have an imposition bank on which they can draw at will. Ask the Head in to restore order? This only confirms them in their belief that they have the respective teachers 'on the run'. So far no one has asked them why they do this with one or two particular men. Why not do so? With-draw them from lessons and let them talk to a counsellor, who will listen and discuss the matter sensibly with them, not emotion-ally but coolly as a member of the same community. This takes time. They are losing time in Chemistry, or whatever the subject is. But so much time has already been wasted anyway. They may look upon this exercise as an escape from a lesson they do not like, but we do not know until it has been tried. They may even reach the point at which they say that they have lost so many periods of Chemistry that it is time they went back and did some work. The rest of the class in their absence might have done some work, and the counsellor might have learned something which might enable him to construct a bridge between them and the staff whose lives they have been ruining for so long. Is this a 'soft' approach? Or is it an attempt to replace a conflict by a real exer-cise in adult understanding? We do not know. But not to try it is to overlook the facts of the case; that conventional solutions have failed, that they are gaining nothing from being in the class, which is being wrecked anyway so that other students are suffering, and that the teachers concerned are being driven to distraction. This staff-initiated situation calls for all a counsellor's tact and diplo-macy. In addition to his customary skill as a counsellor this demands from him the ability to balance on the razor's edge between what-ever his counselling view might be and the need to support his colleagues in solving a commonplace and difficult question of class control. The teachers in the case may resent perhaps their own incapacity to cope, which is a sign in their own minds of professional incompetence. The boys' parents may object to their being withdrawn from a class simply because Mr X seems unable to cope. Whether this method of handling naughty pupils is successful depends upon a complete appreciation of a teacher-counsellor's work by his colleagues, and by parents. In due course the students will come to see what he is about, and to realise that periods with the counsellor are not a 'soft option' but a rather searching process. Because the staff-room situation in matters of this kind can sometimes be extremely delicate, and because some staff regard the counselling relationship as intolerable, counselling in these matters should not be undertaken by over-enthusiastic young men. This calls for experienced staff-members as counsellors, whose professional status and skill as teachers is recognised and accepted in the fullest sense: it suggests too that a teacher-counsellor may again be a better guide than a specialist who is remote from the day-to-day problems of the class-room.

Staff-initiated counselling is not a substitute for competent teaching, and it will lose any value it may possess if every time a teacher has some difficulty he sends an offender 'to see the counsellor'. The latter is not a placebo, still less a quack, and results may be slow in coming. Moreover, the teachers concerned will have to co-operate with their counselling colleague by not provoking the offenders when they return to the class. The students will have been asked by the counsellor at some stage to look at the problem of their own self-control. Equally, their teachers must do the same, and not 'ride' the offending students to the point at which they retort angrily once more, so that the counsellor's patient work is undone. Staff-initiated counselling thus makes demands not only upon the counsellor himself, but also upon his errant clients and those of his colleagues who are concerned in the case. It may fail because of the pupil's inadequacy, the intransigence of teachers, or the counsellor's lack of skill and insight, but no harm will have been done by trying it, for the situation could scarcely be worse than it was before the counselling began. It may on the other hand restore slowly but surely some sort of harmony. It may reveal strains in the client's background which were not even thought of before. It may suggest that outside agencies should be involved. All told it may uncover problems which would never have been displayed if an adult had not taken the initiative rather than waiting for the young client to summon up the courage to do so. It is not a merely pleasant way of ensuring conformity through the medium of a cosy chat away from the more sober realities of the class-room, the subject and a teacher whom the clients do not like. Although it was started on the initiative of a member of the staff, its aims and methods are the same as if the boys themselves had knocked on the counsellor's door of their own volition. Not to use it simply because it was not initiated by the students seems to me to be suspiciously like an evasion of adult responsibility, but great care needs to be used to ensure that it is not used as a new fashion, as an indiscriminately available approach to an old problem.

To discuss these problems is easier than to put solutions of them into effective operation, and it is not difficult to raise obstacles to deploying scarce teachers elsewhere than in the class-room, and to spending time, as the sixth-form group suggested, extravagantly on the needs of those whose reactions might be such that the results were not worth the effort. Counselling, however, can take the strain out of difficult circumstances; and difficulties which argue for themselves so forcibly can often be swept away if the will to try new methods exists. It seems to me, therefore, that counselling might well be more widely used instead of punitive correction with some difficult and unusual cases in schools.

The real issue here again is that unusual cases are not proper bases on which to erect general principles, and much criticism of counselling rests upon consideration of unusual and difficult students. In the present educational climate, counselling is suspect, experience is slight and there are few counsellors. Moreover, the public view of the teacher is still that he should stand in front of his pupils, impart knowledge and impose discipline. More enlightened opinion suggests that if more time was given to counselling, with the help of specialist agencies, and less to standing and talking, knowledge might be gleaned more effectively and assiduously by the students themselves, and the need for corrective punishment of what is fundamentally immature behaviour might abate. Of this we cannot be certain, for in our handling of young people in school we are in an interregnum as old ideas are challenged and new ones are regarded with a somewhat persistent and pragmatic doubt. Moreover, teachers do not accept change with enthusiasm; they often view, with rather more than the critical eye of the research scientist pondering his results, any new ideas which are presented for their attention. My own experience is that counselling relieves student stress and anxiety, improves attitudes to study and the school community, and thus contributes significantly to better performance in work and more co-operative conduct. It turns the student's attention to himself and his own failings; it does not seek to excuse these by suggesting that it is always somebody else's fault that he is as he is or cannot cope with life as it is; it is always concerned with helping him to come to terms with himself as he is and his circumstances as they are; it helps the clients to understand the reasons for their attitudes and behaviour so that they can correct their own faults, if anyone can. The counselling teacher who has to cope with the problems of work and discipline, when all is said and done, has to depend solely on the humanity of his judgement as to how far he can continue to employ counselling principles when there is no helpful response from the client – and there will always be those who respond not at all. He alone has to decide whether, in a given case, he has done all he possibly can with his own resources and his capacity to accept clients' rejection of him, with the skills available to him in external agencies, and within the context of the school in which he works. When he has so decided, he is then entitled to use those resources which are available to him as part of his teaching function to support other student members of the school community, and not in angry frustration, or personal indignation, but in cool appraisal of the special problems presented by the particular student whose difficulties have brought the situation about. But to fall back upon his powers as a formal teacher is his last resort: it is no part of a counsellor's *modus operandi* to use this as anything other than the last remaining weapon in his armoury of skill, patience and his will to understand someone else. If he does use this last weapon, he must explain his reasons to the client.

Before leaving the thorny problem of work and discipline as they are related to counselling, some comment may be appropriate about the relationship between these and teaching techniques. Much is said today about the merits and demerits of streaming and not streaming, about teaching groups which are homogeneous in terms of intellectual ability and those which have a wide ability range. If classes fall into the latter category at which level should the teacher's approach be directed? This question assumes that students have to be 'taught' at all times; it is frequently asked by teachers, and it overlooks entirely the possibilities opened by the use of group working in classes of mixed ability. In such a class of thirty adolescents, for example, we might expect to find several group types: there are those who are bright and capable of working on their own, those who are less bright but still capable of working on their own as long as they have the opportunity of consulting the teacher when they are in difficulty, which may be fairly frequently; there are those for whom any sort of study is difficult, although their attitude to work is excellent; and lastly, there are those whose attitudes to work and school, or to the particular teacher, are bad, and who constitute an element which disturbs the whole of the class. The first three groups present no real problem, except that of deciding the sort of examination or other assessment which is appropriate, as long as help is available for them when they want it. But the fourth group is the root of much trouble that occurs in mixed ability classes. The teacher who counsels is equipped to deal with these people in private interview, either singly or as a group of four or five; he can encourage them to look at their own motives, at why they are a disturbing element to their fellow students. They may not increase their interest in his subject; he may not succeed in eliciting any response; one or two will continue patterns of behaviour, the roots of which lie in the influences to which they are subject outside school and which they cannot resist because of their own personality structure. They will, however, have had some opportunity of understanding that they are regarded as people of value in their own right; that the differences between them and their fellows do not put them beyond the pale. More than this, their fellows will be able to press on with their work, and as long as the teacher-counsellor makes himself available to help them, they will have no resentment. There is not much difference between this situation and the staff-initiated counselling already discussed, but its special significance lies in demonstrating the close link between the two functions of the teacher-counsellor: the teacher who sees the needs of his whole class and the counsellor who uses his special skills to cope with particularly difficult students in it. It suggests the possibility that counselling attitudes can penetrate the orthodox teaching relationship. It is true that it calls for some degree of organisation in the class-room setting, but it should not be beyond the capacity of a teacher to assess the intellectual ability and personal self-control of his class members, to sort the class into groups, and to vary his approach according to these qualities, by giving those who can drive themselves the opportunity to do so while he gives aid which is appropriate to the needs of all. Whatever energy he expends in organisation is saved by using the energy of those who can progress fast on their own at their own level. For the wholly inadequate and the pathological there are other sources of help. For the teacher himself the question he must answer is whether he has to teach the whole class to satisfy his own personal and professional conscience, or whether he can assess the several needs of his students and act appropriately. Suitability for counselling may be decided by the decision he reaches.

One of the most apt comments upon the supposed conflict between the co-operative counselling approach and the formal disciplinary methods of the more traditional teacher was made during a discussion with some young teachers in their last year of training. One of them talked about her experiences in a tough secondary modern school, as she described it. After a few days in the school she found herself engaged in informal after-lesson discussions with some of her students, mainly about the generation-gap between teenagers and their elders. She was herself not long out of her own teenage problems and this, she felt, was probably the reason for them approaching her. My own view was that she also had the right sort of personality to attract them. They talked freely, and what they said she kept to herself in spite of questioning by some members of the staff, a questioning she was able rather vaguely to turn aside, although she was warned about the dangers of this kind of informal relationship. Her comment was to the effect that this informality disposed of, once and for all, problems of discipline. The respect for her which these informal chats engendered continued into the class-room and her student-teaching time, so often a period of considerable trial and difficulty, became extremely relaxed and happy from the time that these informal talks began. In addition, their attitude to and performance in work improved. This young lady was not counselling in the deeper sense but she was making a relationship with her students as individuals not as between pupil and teacher, between worse and better, younger and older, or less intelligent and more intelligent. That relationship carried over into the class-room, because she was interested and concerned about them. What appeared to be a duality of role was in fact two variations on a single theme, depending upon the conditions – the class-room or informal chat – which applied at any given time, a variation which her students understood and accepted too. Her ability, on the face of things, to play two parts was itself the solution to the supposed conflict between them and a tribute to her own maturity. Given, therefore, the appropriate personal qualities in the teacher-counsellor, it seems to me that there is in fact no conflict between the two functions in the discipline and work sense, unless it lies in the lack of confidence of the teacher himself

to discharge the two roles. The students can accept it, certainly in
the middle and later teenage years, without any difficulty, provided that the teacher shows that he can. If he attempts to behave
as the friend and confidant in one set of circumstances and then
treats his students as trash in another by being rude and truculent
himself, clearly he is not able to play two parts and should not try
to do so. But if he treats them and expects them to treat him with
the same courtesy in the public glare of the class-room as he does
in counselling or private conversation, then he can play the two
roles, and his conventional teaching problems will disappear.

6. EFFECTS OF COUNSELLING UPON RELATIONS WITH PARENTS AND SCHOOL GOVERNORS

At several earlier stages in this book I have referred to the view
which may be taken by parents and higher authority. The latter
includes governors, committees and administrators. That this is
important needs no demonstration. The Schools Council, further
education establishments and certain psychologically orientated
bodies like the National Association for Mental Health stand high
in the hierarchy of education, but their influences are to some
degree remote from the hurly-burly of school life and organisation, and less interest is evident nearer the individual school level,
where the views of the local community are significant. A considerable proportion of the adult lay population thinks about
education, consciously or subconsciously, in terms of its several
recollections of personal experiences at school years ago, when
more forcible methods of school control were accepted as normal,
when teaching was more direct and experiences disciplined by
economic factors which have to a large extent been mitigated by
social policy in the last two decades. The subtler techniques of
guidance, advice and counselling were scarcely thought of in
those days. These people are, moreover, much influenced by more
modern status symbol pressures, particularly the need for results in
examinations, which were once the penance of a few and are now

almost ubiquitous. Given a choice between securing examination results, and new educational techniques which might be suspected of interfering with established methods of achieving them, parents and others will tend to choose the former. This choice is based upon the unsubstantiated belief that the two alternatives are mutually exclusive. This, I contend, is not the case. As I have tried to show, counselling is intended to aid the whole development and maturity of the adolescent client, including his intellectual powers; and prejudices, which stem from educational habits devoted to the creation of an academic élite, should not blind us to this intention. There are in my own records several examples of young men, who, in their earlier adolescent years, showed little academic promise, but through the encouragement offered by counselling techniques were able to develop the total personal resources necessary to achieve academic attainment, which was high by any standards. Their later success demonstrated how false and wasteful would have been a rejection based upon formal attainment at age fifteen or sixteen.

Nonetheless, suspicion of this new approach is a natural human reaction in an educational system which is increasingly bedevilled by a jargonised and esoteric complexity almost beyond the understanding of a generation, many of whom were nurtured on marks and punishment alone. They may indeed welcome the humane effacement from the educational scene of sometimes blind and arbitrary corporal punishment: but neither this, nor the suggestion that the academic successes of some brilliant students in the past may have been bought by the educational rejection of many others, can dispel this suspicion. Thus, parents, governors, and members of education committees may well ask what counselling is, and be bemused by the fact that it is not definable in crisp and perspicuous terms. To the uninitiated it must seem vague and ambivalent, even immoral in its acceptance of erring clients, despite my earlier explanations. I have something to say later about the morality of counselling, as distinct from its methods and potentialities, but the crucial issue at the present juncture in our discussion of counselling is the relationship between counsellors and the adult world which provides and sustains the school in which they and the students work. Establishing this relationship is jeopardised by the very obscurity of the counsellor's methods and the imponderability of his results. To treat students with compassion and understanding is to invite so often the charge of being 'soft' with them; not to produce measurable results is to incur doubt. Yet there are fields related to counselling which offer some hope. In education in personal relationships, and in sex education, which demand near-counselling approaches, it is possible to indicate fairly precisely what we hope to achieve. Both these activities involve parental and administrative co-operation and consent. It is rarely withheld and generally parents actively welcome these school initiatives. Moreover, when governors and committees are involved, as they have been by those authorities who have embarked on schemes of these sorts, they have given their whole-hearted support. To gain parental and committee approval, however, requires as clear an exposition as is possible of the aims and processes of counselling, so as to dispel that ambivalence, which derives, on the one hand, from an awareness that the youngsters need help to avoid unhappiness and possible deprivation, and on the other from the possibility that this may be an expensive use of valuable school time; and not only good briefing, but also personal contact with those who discharge the exacting work of the counsellor is needed. It is at the personal level, with his Head, with his governors, with his committee and administrators, and with parents that the good faith of the counsellor is established. For this is the nub of the matter – good faith. It has been said that the relationship between teachers and their employers must at root be based on good faith and mutual trust, simply because much school work is not of such a definitive sort as can be written into a formal contract. This is even more true of the counsellor's work. Parents, and the others

I have mentioned, need to meet and talk with these counsellors who may be deeply concerned in their adolescents' affairs, and hear much about their family troubles, or what they imagine these to be. These people have a right, it seems to me, to satisfy themselves that teacher-counsellors are mature, integrated and discreet people, who are aware of their special responsibility. The meaning of the seal of confidence must be explained to them: reassurance must be given that no detriment to them or the children can possibly ensue; that the purpose is to sustain the family rather than replace it. They need to know that if the clients want outside help and agree to it being sought, parents will be informed if it is possible to do so without breaking the bond of trust between counsellor and client; that the interests of the clients always come first.

Parents and others fully understand the direct use of vocational guidance, the function of careers masters and help in choosing appropriate courses in further education. Much of this work is informal. Despite this it is accepted nowadays as a proper part of school activity, and, to avoid any feeling of exclusion, parents are kept informed and invited to participate. These school functions, like EPR and sex education, are not unconnected with counselling, although they contain elements of direction from the beginning, or offer a set of choices, and they do not present quite as much risk of invasion of family privacy as counselling may entail of which parents may rightly be acutely sensitive. The parents of the clients in Cases 1 and 2 in Chapter I might have been most disturbed by the disclosures and criticism which emerged during the interviews despite their outcome, which in Case 2 was eminently family-sustaining, and indeed thoroughly resentful that a teacher had listened to them without reporting them. On the other hand, we seem to have to accept the fact that adolescents are more often than not readier to talk with someone outside the family circle, because they feel that this person is not as emotionally involved in the domestic problems as parents are. This is a fact of life which parents and others have, I think, to accept, although they may experience some feeling of rejection and being unwanted at first. Parents who are adequately informed, as I indicate in Chapter V, accept this situation easily, and seem to be glad that someone else whom they have met and whose *bona fides* they appreciate is sufficiently concerned to help their children by private conversation and trust him to use this trust wisely, with some humility and a sense of responsibility. Indeed, they see it as a support to their families, not as a substitute which they resent, or an innovation to which they object.

A young probationer teacher, like an earlier example, in a secondary modern school in a rather declining industrial area, started a project on the theme of love. She suggested for her students' consideration various aspects of this, among them love of parents and for parents, love for pets, the love of Christ, the love of beauty in music and the arts generally, and, as one might expect, the love between boy and girl. A parent of one of her students, all of whom were fourteen to fifteen years of age, heard about this idea very early in its development, and the first that the Head of the school knew of it was an irate school governor telephoning her and the angry parent calling to see her, both full of complaint about it. The Head reprimanded the probationer and told her to stop this unseemly project immediately. The girls themselves, I should add, had taken to the idea with evident enjoyment and respect, for here was a teacher not far removed from their age who was beginning to find out how they felt, and thus to understand their emotions. The Head of the school was wrong, in my view, however angry she may have been at not having prior knowledge of the scheme, to take the action she did without proper enquiry and sensible advice, without any attempt at explanation to her mentors or to the young enthusiast. The latter, too, was at fault, in not mentioning to her Head that this was what she intended to do: it did not cross her mind, in her enthusiasm, that anyone could possibly take exception to the

theme of her series of lessons: she did not anticipate that to mention the love between boy and girl is still to rouse some older
people to fury. Why they react in this way is beside the point:
it may indicate that the parents and the governor in this case were
genuinely worried about what was going on, or that they needed
some kind of counselling themselves. But the fact is that such
people do exist, and however stupid advocates of counselling or
similar services may believe such people to be, they have a right
to explanations of what is going on in schools with their children.
No one should deny them this right. If the young teacher had
explained carefully to her Head what she wished to do, how she
intended to treat the subject, and what she had in mind in embarking upon it, the Head could then have taken the sensible step of
calling the parents of the girls in the class concerned together and
explained everything to them, and won them over, if they needed
winning over, to her side. She could have written to them instead.
She could also have given her young protégée some useful advice
perhaps. If she had refused to do either of these she would only
have displayed her own inadequacy and inability to accept responsibility, as was her duty, for an interesting project, which was
likely to be very beneficial to the girls.

This episode indicates the harm which may be done and the
frustration which can arise if care is not taken over communication with parents and governors and authorities. Parental objections and governors' complaints were aroused which could have
been avoided. In this instance it was traceable to the young inno-
vator's lack of experience, and her failure to appreciate the sensitivity of other adults to this kind of new idea. Her experiment was
not one in counselling, but it was approaching it perhaps: it was
certainly getting very near to something which parents feel is
really their responsibility. For this reason she should have communicated better than she did; the Head should not have rebuffed
her young teacher's ideas, but should have used the enthusiasm
and idealism more constructively, and taken an excellent oppor-

tunity to guide her protégée in matters of communication and tact.

I have dealt hitherto with the attitude of parents to counselling, it is also necessary to consider ways of dealing with criticism of parents by clients. This is bound to occur in a good counselling relationship, and it cannot be dismissed as irrelevant or beyond a counsellor's interest. That it has come from the client suggests, but not inevitably, strain between home and school, a not uncommon problem with which many teachers are already well acquainted. Sometimes it is uttered with some reluctance, because the client feels a deep loyalty to his home, yet is aware of the disharmony between school values and what he observes on the domestic scene. At other times it is yet another device to test the counsellor's reactions: yet again it stems from a momentary exasperation, a temporary rebellion against some recent parental edict or prohibition. A counsellor can help here by discussing the reasons for the parents' attitude and helping his client to look at the parents' position, to understand that they care for him, to think about his friends whose parents appear to be experiencing difficulties similar to his own, or others whose parents seem to take no interest at all in their offspring. Everything depends on the case details presented to a counsellor, but he should never impose his view of the parents' attitude. To condemn them may be to arouse intense feelings of family loyalty in his client; to agree with them can cause him to retire from counselling for good. A counsellor may be questioned, as I have often been, about his own relations with his family, and he needs to answer sincerely and diffidently, without being pompous or dogmatic. Always he seeks to help his client to look calmly at his own circumstances, to come to terms with and overcome domestic problems, not to tell him what to do or rush in with help which may make matters even worse. No parent likes to be told, 'Mr X at school said I was to do so-and-so', except in matters of school work.

Sometimes criticism of his home by a client reveals serious

domestic difficulties: marriage stress, a frightening atmosphere, illness, alcoholism. These make the counsellor's task more difficult. Home disturbance of this sort is often long-term, needing remedies beyond a teacher-counsellor's powers. Other agencies are better equipped than he is, and he should know where they can be found, but he must await his client's approval before seeking specialised help in this as in other matters. Some teachers, who are already acquainted with the suffering caused by serious home difficulties, not all of which is uncovered by existing teacher-student relationships, feel strongly that they should involve themselves in direct help, by home-visiting. I do not think that is a counsellor's function, but, if the client wishes, the co-operation of a home-visiting colleague, who can help at the parents' end of the relationship, can be invited, instead of involving the counsellor, whose capacity to counsel the client may be impaired by an emotional concern with the family. There is a distinction to be made here between active practical help to the family and sustaining the spirit and will of his client. These are two distinct functions of equal value, but not, I think, to be discharged by the same person. They call for different qualities.

Parents will, at first, and understandably, object in principle to the possibility that their children may criticise them to their teachers. They do not so often object to their own criticism of their offspring's teachers, however – an action which frequently causes conflicts in the minds of the children concerned. Teachers, however, accept this as part of their professional life, and as they may be acclimatised to the kind of professional difficulties which may arise in counselling, so too may parents be attuned to accepting the idea of their children blowing off steam in the privacy of a counselling room. They should be helped to understand that this is not a species of professional one-upmanship by their children's teacher-counsellor but part and parcel of the whole business of understanding the student client. As in other problems, resolving the problem of non-co-operative or dubious parents turns upon proper communication about a counselling service with parents. They, however, have the right to instruct their children never to use the service, although I would think that this would be an unfortunate decision.

Counsellors will hear adverse comments about other representatives of the establishment; police and clergy for example. This frequently occurs in normal class discussion anyway and undue fuss should not be made about it. A counsellor's task is to help his client to understand the place in society which these people occupy, the difficulties they have to face and how they resolve them. He is not their advocate and should not act as such.

I began this chapter with six questions, which can be summarised and restated in the form of six propositions:

1. There is a difference between a counsellor's responsibility to his client and a teacher's responsibility to his school and authority.

2. He must be prepared to accept criticism of his colleagues and superiors and the implied criticism of himself.

3. He must keep his interviews confidential.

4. He must be prepared for clients who may take advantage of a private and special interview to indulge their own feelings by stating their opinion of him.

5. Counselling may have a complex effect on the general work and discipline of a school.

6. Parents, governors and local authorities may not always share his enthusiasm for counselling.

I have tried to suggest possible lines along which the problems presented to a teacher-counsellor by these propositions can be solved separately. This separation is, however, arbitrary and should not obscure the essential unity between all of them. I believe that the answers to all of them contain either or both of two basic elements. The first of these is fundamentally concerned with the sort of person a teacher-counsellor is; whether he has the personal qualities which enable him to adjust to the needs of different people and the circumstances in which he finds them;

I

the scale of values which determines his attitude to other people. If a teacher-counsellor cannot come to terms serenely within himself with the varying stresses, worries and dilemmas of his various activities no one else can do so for him. The greater part of the burden of making counselling an acceptable educational service therefore falls upon him. This element therefore is closely bound up with problems of selection and training, and with what I call the morality of counselling, the personal-moral view he takes of his work. The second element is relational and communicational, for answers to some of the questions depend upon everyone else connected with a school which runs a counselling service, parents, staff, governors and the local authority, being adequately informed about the aims and methods of the service and the character of the people who are the practitioners.

The problems in the first four propositions depend for their answers largely upon the personal qualities of the individual teacher-counsellor, his attitudes to others, his scale of values. These he must accept as part of his terms of reference, or not counsel. The element of communication is relatively unimportant here, although not entirely absent. This second element, however, is much more significant in the last two propositions: for, even if the right sort of people are available to counsel, their aims and methods are likely to be misunderstood or viewed with considerable suspicion if everyone concerned is not properly informed beforehand. We therefore need the right people to counsel and a sufficient degree of communication with everyone else concerned. Either without the other renders the whole counselling operation nugatory.

Any attempt to help young people to grow into responsible adults must take proper account of the feelings of other adults, parents, administrators, elected representatives and others, all of whom, we must assume, take their responsibilities seriously. If we are not painstaking and tactful in this matter, counselling and cognate services towards personal development will be rightly regarded as interlopers into what many believe are the private preserves of family life, or usurpers of those rights, instead of being seen, as they ought to be seen, as supporters of those rights. Parents and others may be suspicious of new methods, especially those which reveal, on occasion, deep and intimate details of personal and family life: it is the duty of those who advocate these methods to explain them fully, not to take over existing rights and responsibilities arbitrarily. That the Newsom and Albemarle Reports called for further attention to education of the whole person, that their opinions tally with those of other enlightened organisations, does not of itself justify the summary imposition of systems and services by impersonal officialdom. The really significant evidence supporting the introduction of counselling and similar services in schools lies not in official reports but in the demands which are made upon schools by ordinary people, and especially by parents who so often want more help than schools are able to give, and who, when new approaches are explained to them, welcome them as a support to their own hopes and ideals rather than administrative fiats. Given their support, the teacher-counsellor, if he is properly selected and trained, will find that most of his problems will disappear. To organisation and communication and to selection and training I now turn, in that order, in the two following chapters.

SUMMARY

Counselling presents a variety of problems. Some of these are for the counsellor to solve; in his relations with his colleagues and with parents and those who administer the school in which he works; by his ability to distinguish what is said in the counselling room from the more public view he takes of his students in his formal work. Others involve ethical and moral issues, as well as family situations, which everyone connected with the school needs to understand. Yet others are closely connected with his own attitude and demeanour. All are soluble. Although this educational art is new, and still viewed with some doubt, there is a growing body of opinion and social demand, which advocates its extension. Personal experience suggests that its results although not quantifiable are beneficial. The extent to which it becomes accepted and recognised by everyone concerned with secondary education depends upon the efficacy and clarity of communication between all those involved and the selection of counsellors whose personal integrity is not only beyond doubt but is also seen to be so.

IV. Administration and Organisation

Although counselling is a service devoted exclusively to the needs of individual people, or groups of them, it has to be woven into the external fabric of relationships of which a school is a part together with parents, governors and local authorities; it must also fit into the internal relationships of the teaching staff. Some care is needed to avoid unnecessary friction. Moreover, physical arrangements, of space and time, have to be made, as well as facilities for keeping records. We shall look at the physical arrangements first.

ACCOMMODATION AND FURNISHING

This need not be lavish. A small lockable room is all that is required, preferably away from the main streams of school traffic so that its quiet conduces to clients' peace of mind, and the counsellor is not easily disturbed by intrusions. The current design tendency to equip class-rooms in new schools with small offices or stores offers one possible solution to the accommodation problem, but the room must be large enough to accommodate three or four people if necessary. It must be as soundproof as possible. The room needs three or four chairs. Round-backed wood or plastic items will suffice; these are rather more comfortable than routine school chairs and are easily moved. Expensive leather-covered armchairs are unnecessary and lend a quite superfluous air of luxury to the proceedings. The counsellor himself creates the atmosphere, not his furniture, given privacy and a minimum of creature comfort which makes clients feel relaxed. The counsellor will also need a plain but well-finished table and filing cabinet, the key to which he must keep in his possession.

A lockable card index cabinet is sufficient as will be seen when we discuss record-keeping. A telephone is unnecessary: it is a source of interruption, and if the counsellor has to use one to contact outside help he should be able to use the school installation because his client will almost certainly have agreed by this stage to the Head being told of what his problem is. It does not matter whether the room is used for some other purpose by the counsellor or not, as long as no one else uses or has access to it in his absence. The notion that it should be decorated expensively, its walls hung with artistic reproductions and its floor littered with office paraphernalia, is simply mistaking form for substance, of superficiality for reality. It ought to be cheerful, clean, and neat, because this gives a good impression to outsiders – for example, parents who may be called in if occasion warrants – and a scruffy room will scarcely encourage them to have faith in the counsellor. Luxury may be equally disconcerting to them. If this sounds rather spartan it is because we need to explode any idea that counselling and allied services predicate spending large quantities of money and that expenditure on purely material accessories is a substitute for suitable counsellors. There has been at times a tendency among those interested in education to show off lavishly equipped spaces and structures, because these are easily displayed to the advantage of the providers, when the really significant provision, so often neglected or unobtainable, is that of the appropriately competent and enthusiastic people to use them. This sort of window-dressing has no use in counselling.

APPOINTMENTS

Making appointments is clearly a function of the availability of the counsellor, and there are two schools of thought about this. The first postulates that the counsellor should be available at certain specified times on certain specified days in each week. All his intending clients have to do therefore is go and see him during these times. This is extremely tidy administratively, and the counsellor knows that his dual identity is clearly indicated; at certain times of his working week he is teaching, at others he is counselling. The two roles are separable in time as well as in his own mind, and the strains on him are minimised by knowing what he will be doing at one time or another. There is one almost overriding objection to this system. It neglects the feelings of the client entirely, for although an administratively tidy counselling system of this kind is necessary perhaps for adult counselling services or in further education, it may be less suited to the needs of adolescents, and it assumes that their needs only bubble over at times when the counsellor is available. In fact they tend to act quite spontaneously and suddenly think, or so it appears to me, 'I'll go and see ——', usually, I suspect, referring to the man by his current soubriquet in the school. At that moment in time they make their decision, and act upon it. If they do not act upon it at that time, they usually never act on it at all. This rather capricious approach by intending clients creates difficulties when it comes to organising the service. For example, at the time they come he may be about to start a lesson with a formal class. All he has to say to them is something like this: 'I would like you to talk to me very much. The trouble is that I have a class now, which makes it difficult for me to give you the attention you need, and in any case it would be more private if there was no one else in my classroom while we were talking in the office. I am free at . . .' He gives the client some alternatives and they agree a time at which the client shall come. All else he needs to say is 'I look forward to seeing you at . . ., and I shall expect you then.' I have never known an appointment so made not to be kept. I have often speculated how far a client has been encouraged by the fact that I was able to show interest and concern although there were obviously other pressing duties awaiting my attention. Presumably, if the person a client wants to see is apparently not upset by having to cope with several problems at the same time, he is not likely to be easily upset by anything that a client says during counselling. This 'casual' system seems to me to have much to commend it, because it suits better the sometimes evanescent needs of adolescent clients, for whose benefit the system exists. Although continuous availability, at least for making appointments, seems on the face of things rather strenuous, it should not put any additional burden upon a counsellor who is equal to his task. In practice the real distinction between the casual and the organised systems lies in the counsellor's school timetable: the former system makes it quite unnecessary for a counsellor's teaching timetable to be specially arranged, as long as he has some periods scattered through the week for this service. Any service which can be fitted into a normal school timetable without intricate complications has much to commend it; moreover the service looks more normal and less unusual when it is so arranged. Remembering appointments requires only a small book which a counsellor must keep in his pocket and never leave lying about for others to peruse, and it should include only the clients' names, the dates and the times. The less he puts on paper the better. One small matter seems almost superfluous, but teacher-counsellors can be late for appointments for very good school reasons, and whatever the client's age a quiet word of apology is never amiss. For the youngster, it may be a salutary experience – the first time that an adult has ever apologised to him. If he is so late that the client has departed, it is the counsellor's duty to find him, apologise and make a further arrangement.

If a client wants an appointment urgently it may be necessary to see him during one of his normal lessons, and the burden of arranging this must fall upon the counsellor. It is his business to talk to the master who would normally expect the client in his lesson and explain why he will not be there, and he should follow this through when the interview is over by either accompanying the boy back to his class or giving him a note saying simply that the youth was with him and state the times involved. This may seem to be an excess of protocol, but it helps to make his work acceptable to those who may suspect him of undermining their authority, and if a counsellor does not display these fundamental courtesies we cannot expect his non-counselling colleagues to be as sympathetic to his work as they should be. Moreover, it encourages one's teaching colleagues, as well as the clients, to understand that counselling is not regarded as an escape from the more conventional tasks and courtesies of school life. In these small ways school relations can be kept harmonious, and the counsellor's function be seen as contributing to the total life of the school, as one of a team rather than a rather aloof specialist.

RECORDS

Certain confidential records are kept in files about every student in a school. As a general rule these are available for perusal by any member of the staff who wants to look at them. They are confidential in the sense of being confined to the view of staff and parents, rather like school reports. They are not for anyone's glance. A counsellor's records are in a different category: they are for him alone, unless the client agrees otherwise. Even if the client gives his assent to disclosure of the private information he has supplied, the counsellor's records should not be put into the confidential school file, to which I have just referred. This information, even if disclosure to a specified person has been agreed by the client, may be important only to the Head of the school, or to the student's house or year master. It clearly helps here if the latter is also the counsellor concerned. It is not for general information for the whole staff, not all of whom may be in any degree counselling-orientated or sympathetic to the kind of sociological and home difficulties which emerge during counselling. If any guidance about this is needed for the whole staff, a general note from the Head or house or year master stating that so-and-so has considerable difficulties to cope with and should be sympathetically handled is sufficient. There is no need for any member of the staff to mention this to the student, who may be very embarrassed by any hint that his difficulties, even if not known in detail, are common knowledge among the staff.

Counsellor's records should themselves be as brief as possible. I find small index cards sufficient. I number them and keep a small book separately which links these numbers with the names and forms of clients. This is perhaps carrying security to an almost ridiculous limit but privacy in my mind is sacred. The notes I inscribe on cards are minimal, just sufficient to recall to mind the kind of difficulty which the client presented and what came out as the interviews developed. For example, Case 2 in Chapter I was recorded as follows:

Not allowed to stay out late, even for church functions
Mother an invalid
Talked to church member
Client returned; NFA (no further action)

and Case 1

Girl friend trouble – not pregnancy: thrown out of home
Bad relations with parents on both sides
Suggested living together
Suggested following agencies for his action: House of help;
Probation service: to let me know when to intervene
Continued counselling; Head informed; NFA

and Case 6

Dispute with Mr X: injustice
Acted as intermediary; NFA

and Case 5

Wants psycho. treatment: depression–elation
Staff, school and parents in disrepute
Talked Dr Y (consultant) privately – to wait and see
Client happy at second interview – had someone to talk to; NFA

and Case 4

Further education bother: expectation exceeds ability
Family ambitions at stake

(handled this one badly at first)
Client came to terms at third talk; NFA

Such brevities, with a number at the top, tell nothing to anyone into whose hands they might wrongfully fall. Even the addresses I omit, for these are in the school's usual files. I find these brief notes absolutely adequate, but others might think it useful to add a little more: for example at the end of the first interview with a client it might be helpful to add a note which indicates a possible line of further progress in the second one, so that some kind of continuity is maintained. Too much, however, is dangerous, for, as I suggested earlier, some of the information which emerges is highly explosive social material. I never write notes while I am actually counselling: my clients know that I shall keep some sort of record, because at an appropriate moment in the first interview, when they are more relaxed, I tell them this, but explain that these are for my eyes only. Making notes with adolescent clients distracts them and makes them suspicious, I find, as indeed it seems to do when counselling adults in other situations.

I ought to emphasise at this stage that I am concerned only with records for personal counselling. More sophisticated practitioners who are involved with sociometric and psychometric testing or with careers guidance of necessity have to keep more detailed records perhaps, and much of their information will have to go into the school file. In the future, as counselling services develop and allied activities, such as home-visiting by teachers, grow, some sort of centralised record-keeping systems might be required, but personal counselling is much less concerned with data, graphs and statistical information, and records based on it should be kept apart. I should not like to see the time come when over-elaboration of records leads to depersonalisation and less privacy. The person only matters, not how his records are kept: his problems mean more than the administrative machinery. Whatever records are kept by a counsellor, they should be seen only as a means to the client being helped more effectively, not as an end in themselves, and counsellors should not devote time to paper which should be given to people.

RELATIONAL PROBLEMS

a. *External*

Already we have laid considerable emphasis on the need to communicate with parents and others about the methods and aims of a counselling service, and suggested that some of the difficulties which might be expected can be destroyed at their origin by a sensible and courteous dissemination of information. The responsibility for this is essentially a Head's, and what follows therefore depends upon his own understanding of and faith in such a service. Clearly, one who does not believe in this kind of approach to adolescent problems will not introduce it into his school. The sequence of action which I suggest therefore assumes his interest and active support, and the existence on his staff of at least one teacher who is selected and trained as a teacher-counsellor.

It does not matter much whether he puts his governors or the parents of his students in the picture first, as long as the relevant meetings take place close togehter. These will need to be special meetings devoted to this topic and not cluttered with a mass of routine other business. The contents and conduct will be similar, except that the parents' gathering will obviously be a larger one. In each meeting, the Head should be accompanied by the teacher-counsellor, who should ideally be someone who is so trusted and respected in the professional teaching sense that his reputation has gone before him and he is already known personally to the governors and to some of the parents at least. Fears of an unknown interloper with new-fangled ideas are thus dispelled: the stranger whom no one knows is always regarded with some uncertainty, and if he brings in his train a rather revolutionary action, as counselling is to many people, then suspicion is more than doubled. Here I should add that a newcomer to a staff who intends to counsel and who may have been appointed with this in view might be well advised to establish himself as a teacher alone before embarking upon counselling. This, I appreciate, is a counsel of perfection but it is wiser to aim at the best than accept the worst in a context as delicate as this.

Both governors and parents should be given a plain statement of intent to introduce a counselling service, followed by a simple description of what this entails. If a Head feels that the latter should be given by the teacher-counsellor himself, so much the better. He is the person who knows what it is all about and for him to explain it also indicates the confidence which the Head has in his choice. It is crucial that he should demonstrate this confidence and that governors and parents should, if they do not know him already, gain a personal acquaintance with the person concerned. The account of counselling can be set against a background of alleged adolescent turbulence; of difficulty in communication across the generations and between parents and children in particular; of the general absence of anyone for young people to talk to, and their feeling that they are inanimate parts of an impersonal social machine; of interest at a high level as demonstrated by the *Schools Council Working Paper*. The audience might be invited to think about their relations with their own children. The essential privacy of counselling should then be stressed: this will raise doubts and misgivings, which may be allayed by asking the doubters whether they would prefer their children to stumble from one crisis – of any sort – to another until they are in real trouble, without the benefit of some private personal help if they want it. This is the point at which to emphasise that this service is not intended to replace parental care and interest by an official procedure nor to imply that parents are incompetent but is instead a potential buttress to parents who are worried, and that it includes encouraging the counsellor's clients to seek their parents' help after they have talked with him, either directly or through an intermediary if necessary. This, it must be emphasised, cannot be enforced and it is of course likely that the clients may take no notice of the suggestion. Parents should know that this may happen. Parents and governors will also need assurance that if their children present any really serious problem, no action will be taken by the school without consulting them, but it is equally important for them to understand that a client who decided to solve his own problems cannot be compelled to inform his parents without breaking the seal of privacy. My experience suggests that this last situation only arises when as in Case I in Chapter I communication between parents and client has ceased anyway. Lastly, parents should know that no one in the school is compelled to undergo examination by a counsellor, that it is entirely voluntary, with the exception of work and discipline problems mentioned in Chapter III, in which a special problem is under investigation; the purpose of counselling is to help to develop the character and ability of clients in the interests of themselves and everybody else.

This is clearly a highly simplified account, and the audience, whether governors or parents, will want to ask questions. Some of these will be trivial, some will be serious, and this is the counsellor's opportunity to display at once his integrity and equanimity, as well as genuine interest in whatever is asked of him, and to say something about his attitude to the work and the kind of selection and training he has had for it. It is imperative that parents and governors understand that counselling is not just something that anyone can do at a moment's notice, and that not all who believe they can do it are necessarily chosen. There is little doubt that, among parents, it will be the appreciative ones who will turn up for a briefing. They may be small in number, yet the fact that the opportunity has been given not only discharges what I believe is a proper duty of a school, but also protects the school from any suggestion that it is on its own initiative interfering with the private lives of its children and their families. The questions parents put and the answers which they are given can help to unite school and parents in a common purpose and may greatly help the latter in adjusting their own reactions to difficulties which so often arise at home when children are in the adolescent years. Parents may indeed seek advice on their own account and teacher-counsellors may sometimes find it useful to counsel them in an effort to help parents to understand their children better. I suggested earlier however that links with parents generally may be better developed through home-visiting teachers or external welfare services.

These essays in communication with people outside the school should not be couched in the jargon of an expert but in simple everyday terms; highly technical phrases bemuse laymen, raise obstacles to good will unnecessarily and stimulate parental anxiety without justification. Teacher-counsellors are not professional psychiatrists and are not looking for disturbed people: they can, however, usefully explain the sources of the specialist help available to them if they feel these are needed. The counsellor's uncomplicated helpfulness is especially valuable at a time like the present, when many students receive an education, in the intellectual sense, of which their parents have little understanding, with the result that the gaps between children and parents yawn so widely as to create in some families a degree of mutual contempt. A teacher-counsellor may not be able to bridge this gap either at all or as effectively as might be wished, but he can help the parties to understand it, not to feel resentful about it and to live with it. His contribution is that he accepts the difference as existing, and copes with it because it is there.

Any meeting with parents or governors demands the presence of a member of the local education authorities staff, so that the local education committee are kept abreast of what is happening. Sometimes it is useful to combine governors' and parents' meetings, and although this can be more taxing to the teacher-counsellor it has the advantage that both parties hear the same account of what is being done in the school and discuss the same problems with the Head and teacher-counsellor together. Such a combined meeting effectively stifles the possibility that any one party will cause trouble by reporting alleged complaints to another without the Head's previous knowledge. This is essentially a team operation, the central figures in which are the Head and his teacher-counselling staff, but whose responsibility has to be supported by the good will, interest and trust of the other parties. The one thing which must be avoided is publicity. Not everyone would perhaps go so far as to say nothing at all about counselling in the letter inviting people to the meetings at which it will be explained and discussed, apart from mentioning that it is proposed to introduce such a service. In my view, however, it is unwise to say more in print than that this service provides an opportunity for students to discuss difficulties of any sort in absolute privacy with an adult. It is, for example, mandatory not to say that students are actively told or ordered to take their personal problems to members of the staff instead of their parents. In the Introduction I expressed the view that some teachers have been appointed to pastoral care posts without any real comprehension of, or preparation for, the kind of emotional difficulties which may come their way. Some teachers are, quite bluntly, totally unsuited to this kind of work; one of the purposes of the meetings is to demonstrate as far as possible the essential suitability of the available teacher-counsellors for the tasks they have undertaken. A delicate confidential service such as counselling is not aided by publicity. Photographs of counselling rooms, with counsellor and student in mock solemn conclave, are a travesty of the values and privacy of counselling; they turn an intimate, personal service into an advertising agency for a particular school. What is essentially private is deprived of this quality by public display. Moreover, the growth of counselling is better aided by quiet and almost intangible evidence from parents and students of its success, by letting it prove itself in the passing of time, not by ghoulish glamour more appropriate to a star of entertainment or by published implications that the mere existence of a so-called counselling service, regardless of who the practitioners are, is itself a guarantee that all the relevant school's problems will vanish. There is ample opportunity for near-clinical appraisal of its value in specialist journals, but advertising its existence, even in a school magazine, reduces this delicate and difficult task to a mere stunt, apart from possible offence to parents. Adolescents who are in difficulties are not proper subjects for stunts, and neither they, their parents nor anyone else should be encouraged in the belief that a single person in the school holds the remedies for an army of adolescent disturbances, most of which are healthily normal and need nothing more than the presence of someone to talk to for a sane return to relative tranquillity. It is wholly unnecessary to state or even imply that they are all in a pathological state or that they will all tell the most horrific tales about their homes. The purpose of this communication exercise with people outside the school is primarily to introduce them to the idea that the school staff contains one or two thoroughly discreet and integrated people who are specially selected and trained to listen, to let people blow off steam, to help them to look at life more sensibly; that they are partners with their teaching colleagues in the complex business of educating the whole person rather than quasi-expert cranks seeking to interfere, in their own interests, in the domestic affairs of their young charges and their families; and that nothing will appear in school reports about anything that transpires in counselling interviews. This is an exercise in good public relations, as distinct from publicity: the former is a requisite of counselling, the latter a disaster.

b. *Internal*

What I have written about conducting external relationships applies equally to relations with the staff. They require the same clear statement, free from alarming overtones, as the parents and governors. Some of them will be dismayed at the thought that one of their colleagues may be the recipient of critical comment, but it scarcely helps to suggest that every client will want to

K

indulge in this, when the number who do so is in fact relatively small, and of that number a negligible proportion will be in any sense serious. A staff's needs are largely those of reassurance of the good faith and integrity of their counselling colleagues and their desire to enhance subject-teacher relations with their students. This is bound to be more difficult in large staffs than it is in a staff of say twenty or thirty. In the latter everyone knows everyone else and much of any harmonisation which is necessary can be accomplished at the level of private conversation through personal knowledge of the character and competence of those who counsel. On the other hand, it is disconcerting to reflect upon the fact that a staff meeting in a large school could be a bigger affair than a parents' meeting in a smaller one. A single counsellor in a large school is in real danger of being a remote and impersonal agency unknown to many of his colleagues. The need for the existence of more than one counsellor in large schools is therefore accentuated: apart from the gains which accrue from two or more counselling teachers being able to discuss their cases together in any type of school, large schools need a counsellor for each administrative unit so that one of them at least is known personally to his immediate colleagues, and each member of the staff has a point of personal contact with at least one teacher-counsellor. In these circumstances there is much to be said for the Head introducing a counselling service to his staff through a preliminary meeting which consists of his Heads of houses or years and the counselling staff only. He can follow this with a series of meetings with convenient sections of the staff in smaller groups in whatever arrangement is convenient and relevant to the organisation of his particular school. The precise mechanics of staff communication in large schools are a matter for Heads to settle. They are less important than developing the right sense of personal relationship and trust between those who only teach and those who counsel in the sense I have described as well.

SUMMARY

Accommodation for counsellor-teachers should be simple, tidy and private, not luxurious or overlooked. Whether a teacher-counsellor's timetable should include specific afternoons or mornings for counselling rather than scattered periods is a matter for internal arrangement: I prefer the latter. In either case he needs to keep an appointment book. Records are totally private and should not, as far as personal counselling is concerned, ever form part of the general school file on any given pupil.

Communication with parents, governors, and staff when a counselling service is first started has to be reassuring rather than alarmist, in plain rather than expert terms and personal rather than procedural, with emphasis on sustaining the family and the subject teacher rather than replacing or denigrating them. The reputation of the counsellor as a person is important, and the problems of communication in large schools may be usefully handled by delegation to Heads of subordinate sections. Publicity of any sort should be avoided, nor should the impression be given that a counsellor is the answer to every problem.

v. Selection and Training for Counselling

anifestly, not all teachers are potential counsellors. What sort of people ought, then, to be chosen from the serried ranks? This we need to know, at least in general terms, before we can look at selection and training methods. Appropriate personal qualities will probably have begun to suggest themselves from what has so far been written, for the work itself, its possible crises and dilemmas, predicate the person.

A counsellor has to tolerate so-called eccentricities of manner and dress, and not be disturbed by the emotional outbursts, mistakes or vehement opinions of his clients. He has to accept criticism of himself and his colleagues on the staff, and comment by his staff colleagues about his work, with good grace and humour. He needs to be equable and at peace with himself, but not inanimate or insensitive. Patience, sympathy, understanding and the ability to see situations as others see them, need accompaniment by an infinite capacity for attentive and thoughtful listening. He must be and be seen to be stable and dependable, and absolutely capable of keeping confidence. He must not regard human problems as abstract intellectual exercises, for he will have to cope with human beings whose feelings are intense, real and important to them, and superficially at least deny plain intellectual analysis. For him to see situations in sharply delineated blacks and whites is little help, for most of his client's problems will be subtly shaded. He must be able to think clearly, although he will have to deal with situations which are not susceptible to cold and impersonal logic. He may have to resist considerable pressure, direct and indirect, to reveal what has been said to him. Such a person is probably, in the broadest sense, highly moral, and he must believe in some scale of personal and social values even if this is not expressible in the formal terms of a traditional faith. Taken as a whole these personal attributes amount perhaps to a prescription for perfection, and if, as I have heard suggested, there are few teachers who possess them in adequate quantity and depth, then this is a poor commentary on the standards of entry to the teaching profession and implies that these need investigation as a separate problem. In any event, however, we have to search for these qualities for no other reason than that the nature of counselling demands them.

Quite apart from the difficulty of recognising the qualitites a counsellor should possess, and selecting those who possess them, a professional problem arises, which may be trivial in essence, but which is a potential source of misunderstanding. There are those who maintain that to select particular teachers and train them for specific educational duties, in which I include counselling, is to make invidious distinctions between people of equal professional status. The argument runs that all teachers are professionally trained and skilled in dealing with the manifold problems which young people present to them, that all are equally competent, and that to select one for a particular function exalts him and denigrates his colleagues. Of course, such an argument may throw a searing light upon the professional competence of those who present it, but it exists and it cannot be dismissed simply by casting aspersions upon its exponents. Selection for counselling is not a selection for promotion or financial reward, and at this point a comment about the financial prospects for counsellors may not be out of place, because a vaguely perceptible pattern of attaching financial rewards to full- or part-time counselling posts is emerging, if advertisements in educational journals are any indication of policy in this respect. Obviously this makes counselling attractive to ambitious teachers who may find it difficult to enhance their incomes by obtaining special allowances in subject teaching or through administrative responsibility. Mercenary motives are not restricted to industry and commerce, and I am rather uneasy at the prospect that purely monetary considerations should govern the selection and training of teachers for a service which is so intensely personal as counselling. The policy of attaching substantial extra emoluments to counselling posts could be disastrous to this service by attracting the wrong people into it, unless it is accompanied by a most rigorous selection procedure. My earlier recommendation that counselling should only be undertaken by teachers of some experience and proven professional merit to some extent obviates this difficulty, for these people will have already begun to move up the rather complicated salary ladder in their own subjects, or in responsibilities as house- or year-masterships, so that their counselling will be seen, not as a step to further money, but as the acquisition of a new skill, with space provided in their timetables to exercise it. If counselling services continue to expand the question of salaries will have to be watched continuously, to ensure that the attractions for teacher-counsellors are based on concern for people not on the prospect of pecuniary rewards.

Selection is therefore a proper first step towards preparation for a duty, the special difficulties and stresses of which earlier chapters have exemplified, not for cash benefits. If it is thought that this makes distinctions between members of a staff, between those selected and not selected, in terms of competence or vague advantages to be gained round and about the school, a brief study of the situation in any school suggests that this fear is quite unjustifiable. For, in any staff-room, every teacher has attributes and capabilities which are peculiarly his own and which contribute, together with those offered by his colleagues, to the total operation of the school. The special gifts and qualities which each individual member of a staff possesses are, or ought to be in a well-organised establishment, used to the best advantage of everyone in it, teachers and pupils alike, without regard to the advantages which are conferred upon him by the tasks he performs outside his usual class-room teaching. Sportsmen, producers of plays, organisers of school journeys abroad, visits to local industries and places of other significance, managers of chess clubs, stamp-collecting and debating societies, and all the other activities which go on in schools – all these people collectively create an atmosphere which is lively and stimulating as part of their functions as teachers. Of course there are the usual grumbles about minor matters which afflict any human society from time to time, but in general these school businesses proceed apace without serious friction or major complaint. Yet, each of them gives its staff-member an opportunity to enhance his reputation, to make relationships with pupils which are distinct assets to his conduct of formal lessons and incidentally help to solve any problems of class control which he may have, simply because his students come to know him better through these organisations. They are part of his job; they make the routine side of that job easier and more relaxed simply because they enable him to create better personal relations with his pupils, who see on these extra-mural occasions another side of a human being they normally encounter only in the class-room. This is a matter of common experience, not only in the minds of teachers and their students, but also in the memory of adults whose school days are far behind them. Successful schools depend upon it.

The special duties and gifts of the teacher-counsellor do not therefore erect any new principle which is fundamentally different, or challenge any existing practice. But the task is a new one in English educational experience and I suspect that it is the implications of deep involvement, however discreet, in the personal affairs of students and their relations with staff colleagues, which arouse misgivings among teachers about selection for counselling. There is a suspicion that counselling necessarily implies better qualities, rather than different. This may of course be shown in the future to be true, and how far the suspicion or the facts of this situation can be allayed will emerge as experience in this country grows. The Gloucestershire scheme for training teachers in Education in Personal Relations and the Birmingham plan for Sex Education do not evade this issue. They insist on selecting teachers for their respective schemes with a stringency comparable to that employed by the Marriage Guidance Council in selecting its voluntary counsellors; and it will suffice to say here that this stringency is severe by any standard. As to the professional doubts and suspicions about selection, the Gloucestershire Education Authority's conclusion is that selection gives confidence not only to those who are selected, but also to those who are not: the former because they feel competent to undertake the exacting work demanded of them; the latter because they realise that their selected colleagues are people who can be professionally trusted not to abuse the privacy and delicacy of their work. It is fair to say that this conclusion is the result of experience in EPR, an experience which dispels the kind of doubts I have already expressed. There is, nonetheless, a residue of opinion that rejection might be professionally damaging, because some appointing bodies might look upon failure to be selected for counselling as an indication of incompetence in orthodox teaching. In my view, however, authorities who are as ignorant as this of the special nature of the work would be unlikely to ask about it, and there is no duty upon a teacher to mention that he has been rejected for counselling when he applies for a conventional teaching post in his subject. One can only dispel this residual opinion by ensuring that selection is careful and thorough, so that counsellors are shown, as EPR teachers in Gloucestershire have been shown, to be equal to the total demands of this new task, and by giving opportunities for those who have been rejected once to apply again at a later date.

It is not enough to be a volunteer for counselling. Enthusiasm and a sort of evangelical fervour are not enough. The National Marriage Guidance Council which controls selection of candidates for voluntary service as counsellors throughout England and Wales, and to whose stringent methods I have already referred, rejects over sixty per cent of those who offer their services, after a searching selection procedure in two parts. I believe that a similar process must be applied to teachers who volunteer. Some volunteers for social and personal service are impelled by a desire to impart a set of virtues or extol a point of view under the impression that this is the same as understanding clients and developing their own resources. Without doubting the motives of such volunteers, their messianic urges are not a recommendation. Those who are reserved and thoughtful, who do not carry their principles and beliefs overtly on their sleeves, may make better counsellors than extrovert devotees to rigid principles, however exalted or inspired these may be. On the other hand, conscripts are worthless for a personal counselling service; this is not a duty to be discharged under compulsion. Later, I suggest possible ways in which a teacher who is contemplating counselling should begin to consider seriously his own potential as a counsellor in a school environment. This is the start of self-selection, before he actually volunteers; because it is the embryo of self-analysis it is probably the best way to approach a counsellor's work.

As we have seen already, the counselling relationship transgresses some established customs of professional conduct. This creates embarrassments and dilemmas, whether they are resolved in the ways suggested in Chapter III or in other ways. A teacher-counsellor cannot brush these professional problems aside, for to do so would imply a loss of that sensitivity to other people's ideas and feelings which is a mandatory part of the counsellor's stock-in-trade. He must be aware of his colleagues' whims and idiosyncrasies before he can counsel in his school context, and help his clients, among other things, to learn the art of adjusting to other people, among whom the counsellor's colleagues are included. A counsellor who expects all his colleagues to think as he does about the difficulties which his clients have simply deceives himself, and self-deception by counsellors is no help to their clients. Moreover his clients certainly know that their counsellor's colleagues do not think as he does about them, and they will tell him so if their relationship with him is what it should be: they expect him to know it too, so that he may be better able to help them sensibly if relationships with other teachers come within the purview of their counselling (Cases 3, 5, 6 and 7 in Chapter I illustrate this), because if he knows this then he is the sort of person who can accept his colleagues' disagreements with him serenely, and thus have some chance of passing on his serenity to his clients.

This situation, working with clients and colleagues who can scarcely be expected to see eye to eye about the same problems, is one of quite acute stress for the counsellor. He must not be disturbed by what amounts to a tug-of-war going on inside him. If he is conscious of it so much the better, for he can come to terms with it, as he must because it is an inescapable part of the teacher-counsellor's daily round. Ability to achieve this inner harmonisation, to live with a stress situation, is not, I think, given to everyone. Some obviously have it; others, sometimes quite unexpectedly, reveal it when the opportunity to do so presents itself; others quite patently lack it. Whatever selection there may be for entry to teaching does not take this much into account, if at all, and the burden of finding candidates who possess this, among other desirable qualities, must form part of any selection procedure which is used to identify potential counsellors. However, before I discuss more sophisticated techniques which are part of the search process, some basic information about candidates for counselling will help to make a preliminary selection.

SELECTION

To start with, a minimum of five years' teaching experience is, in my view, desirable, unless candidates possess exceptional qualities and give proof of unusual and relevant activities. Starting a career in teaching adolescents is not at all easy in a society which rightly looks more and more askance at formal disciplinary sanctions and increasingly burdens its teachers with responsibilities outside the

intellectual sphere. Young teachers have to adjust to these professional conditions and to changing patterns of student needs even
in the formality of the class-room, as well as to continuous changes
in subject-matter, teaching method and educational aims.
Emotional stress and nervous exhaustion are not uncommon
among new entrants to the profession as they try to establish their
reputations in schools, whatever the latter's type or quality.
Moreover, they have not only to adjust to the stress of a new job,
fresh from the at least partial seclusion of life at university or
college of education, they now have responsibility for the total
management of their own personal lives in every sense. This on
its own is quite a complex affair until the individual becomes
attuned to the decision-making it demands. This emergence into
full occupational and private independence and responsibility and
all its corollaries is part of his as yet incomplete maturation, of
coming to terms with himself. It is not infrequently complicated,
nowadays, by early marriage, often to someone in the same stage
of personal development, so that a third dimension of difficulty is
added to the others. This is not a comment on the wisdom or
otherwise of early marriage, but simply on the additional strains
which accompany it. Five years is therefore a fair minimum
period in which it is not unreasonable to expect teachers to adjust
to the changes in their total personal lives and achieve a good
measure of personal integrity, of emotional stability, and of self-
reliance. For some, of course, it may take longer, extending well
past their middle twenties. If this repetitious emphasis on the
maturity of the whole person seems tedious or unfair, it is wise to
bear in mind that many of the intending counsellor's clients may
know more about the hard truths of life than the counsellor himself, because they will come from backgrounds and move into
future occupations very different from the somewhat secluded
and rarefied atmospheres of much conventional further education
– and I am not discounting here the experiences gained by students in finding lodgings and in vacation jobs.

Much of this is possibly at variance with the policy of certain universities and colleges of education, which include a counselling element as an option in their basic teacher training. The content of this element is variable, but seems more often to be directed to social work or careers guidance than personal counselling. This displays a commendable foresight by the course-constructors concerned, in anticipating some of the non-teaching demands which will arise during the professional lives of those whom they train. They may select their candidates for these courses with some care, but they would be wise to ensure that they do not overlook the kind of difficulties I have just outlined in their commendable keenness to keep ahead of events. These young teacher-counsellors may find themselves frustrated by Heads and authorities whom they may think are timid, cautious, or even unsympathetic, when they move into their first jobs. They may find their youth and inexperience of humanity severe handicaps, which make their potential clients reluctant to accept them. They may realise that the traumatic experience of starting to teach and to organise their lives denudes them of the extra resources which their counselling duties demand from them. I would like to feel that caution will be observed in future development of these initial training courses, for it requires an exceptional degree of personal maturity to be able to counsel in any sense at twenty-one years of age. My view, therefore, is that the training of teacher-counsellors should first be directed to mastery of the teacher's conventional skills and knowledge, and that those who wish to do so should, after five years' experience or more, seek additional training in counselling, by which time they will be better able to make a sensible decision about the wisdom and relevance of so doing, in the light of their personal development.

One category of teachers-in-training who constitute a possible exception to this general prohibition are the so-called mature students, who enter college after they have had some experience in other occupations, usually when they are twenty-five or more

years of age. These seem likely to be better candidates for counselling courses very early in their teaching careers and indeed in
colleges themselves than young teachers. Their age, down-to-
earth knowledge of humanity, poise and adaptability are qualities
which many of them already display in their schools and bring
distinction to the teaching fraternity. They are acceptable to
adolescents because they are often well acquainted with the sort
of industrial and commercial world into which the youngsters
will shortly move. Their advice seems relevant because it is borne
out of experience; they tend less to be hampered by professional
customs which they find outmoded and upset by the errors of
others than are teaching recruits who enter colleges at the customary age of eighteen or thereabouts. Some display an uncanny,
even inborn, skill in handling young people and a rare ability to
avoid putting themselves in positions from which they cannot
withdraw gracefully. Their status and reputation does not often
seem to depend as much on the trappings of formal authority as
upon their practical experience of life outside the seclusion of
school. Many of them may make excellent counsellors but they
too must go through a selection process, for it does not follow
that they will all be good counsellor material.

One important question to be answered in assessing counselling-
suitability is that of marital status. Again the ideas of the Gloucestershire Education Authority about EPR teachers are interesting.
Their view is that EPR with adolescents should rest in the hands
of married teachers, although they did not specifically exclude
outstanding unmarried candidates. The Birmingham scheme for
sex education makes no stipulations about this at all. My own
experience of a teacher's course for EPR arranged for staff volunteers in a school in another part of the country is little help here.
There were nine volunteers at the start, of whom three withdrew,
i.e., selected themselves out of the course, at the end of two discussion sessions, and they were the only married ones in the
group! They found self-analysis most difficult and were particu-

larly embarrassed by discussion of sexual problems. Moreover, there are certainly outstanding examples of single people who can give unembarrassed help in sexual matters with conspicuous success. It is thus difficult to draw firm conclusions in this matter from the scanty experience available. Certainly the Marriage Guidance Council specifies that its counsellors shall be married, but theirs is a specialised field, and although their experience and advice is unique and extraordinarily valuable, it does not necessarily follow that their prescription should be rigidly accepted. On balance, it is probably true to say that, of two candidates who in all other respects seem to be of equal potentiality as counsellors, the married one is more likely to be a better counsellor than the single. So much, however, depends on the extent to which any individual, married or single, male or female, has come to terms with the state in which he or she is. The single person who has achieved this and can discuss sexual problems, as every counsellor has to do at some stage, without embarrassment at any remark which may be made, however offensive it may sound in a client's vernacular, will counsel better than the married person who has not. Married status should not therefore be a bar, without reference to other considerations.

Academic qualifications, measured in terms of possessing a university degree, seem to me to be totally irrelevant to this work, and I view with some misgiving any suggestion that personal counselling is only for those with high level and second degrees. Sensitivity to the needs and feelings of human beings seems to be blunted at least as often by intensive academic study as it is sharpened, and merely passing examinations is frequently a desensitising impersonal process. Good academic qualifications may fairly indicate a high level of abstract intellectual acuity, but this is not synonymous with understanding the vagaries of human feelings or the delicacy of human relationships. Those who are intellectually 'bright' frequently find it extremely difficult to understand those who are less bright, or even those who are bright but are experiencing difficulties in personal life. Of course, sensitivity which is accompanied by mental perspicacity is likely to be more useful in helping a client to solve his problems than sensitivity without it: this is not in dispute. In discovering teacher-counsellors, however, we are not searching through the whole population with its intrinsically wide-ranging mental ability; we are sifting a particular section of the population, which has already passed through an intellectual sorting process in its admission and training sequence; and here we may need to remind ourselves that this sequence still is almost wholly dominated by intellectual attainment expressed as college entry qualifications. Thus our candidates for teaching-counselling already possess a reasonable degree of intellectual capability. In searching for qualities of character among them we are looking for attributes which distinguish some people from others of approximately equal intellectual status. It may indeed turn out in the future that people with degrees make better counsellors than those without, or that the better the degree the better the counsellor; but, for the present, there seems to be little evidence of this. I think it inappropriate therefore both to reject potential counsellors because they lack a degree and to accept them because they have one.

Given candidates of the appropriate age and experience who have adjusted to the stresses of teaching and living, and who believe that they can cope with the duality of the counselling role, documentary evidence must be sought to support the applications. If training for teacher-counsellors becomes practical politics, presumably the appropriate selection methods and training courses will become the responsibility of local education authorities as they have become in the cases of EPR. When a course is publicised by a local authority, it therefore seems sensible for intending counsellors to apply through their headmasters, basing their applications upon their professional experience and personal background, and seeking their Head's support. Here we are in a difficulty, even assuming that the appropriate Head is sympathetic to counselling as a school service, for traditional references and testimonials extolling the virtues of examination results, conscientious preparation and marking, and discipline which is firm but friendly are scarcely adequate. They only confirm what may be a mere modicum of professional competence, or conceal mediocrity in the traditional teacher–class relationship. Much more revealing are answers to questions such as those listed below. And any teacher who is interested in counselling might well ponder the answers he would give to these questions about himself before he puts his Head in the position of answering them. In part they cover earlier ground but they constitute a useful beginning to that process of critical self-analysis of which a counsellor must be capable before he can assist his clients.

1. How does he react to criticism? Quickly defensive? Abjectly apologetic? Coolly discursive? Can he listen to and accept advice?

2. Does he seize every opportunity to relate every minuscule achievement of his own? Or every insignificant misdemeanour on his colleagues' part?

3. When asked for an opinion is he facile, verbose, superficial, even obsequious? Or thoughtful, concise, perceptive? Does he try to provide that which he thinks his superiors want, or be objective, or extol the virtues of his opinions?

4. How does he react to crisis, accident, departures from the normal? Is he cool, or does he panic? Will he act upon his own judgement and justify it by the facts of the situation when he is asked to account for his actions, or will he dash for the safety of higher authority?

5. Has he any opinions which he holds dogmatically, to which he can accept no opposition?

6. Does he tolerate fools gladly, or run out of patience quickly?

7. How do his students react to him in those out-of-school activities in which he takes part? Can he alter his relationship easily, and can his students accept the change?

8. Is he relaxed in his control of students in teaching periods and around the school? Or is he easily rattled by momentary disorder?

9. Is he conscientious in discharging routine duties, in punctuality, in tidiness?

10. How loyal is he? To superiors? To subordinates and students?

11. Is his influence on the school community determined by manner, appearance and attitude, or by sanctions?

12. Is he absolutely trustworthy in every facet of his work? In keeping information to himself especially?

This list is not complete, but the answers to these questions, and possible conflicts between answers to different ones, can often throw a searching light on the character and temperament of the man as distinct from the academic instructor. It gives a further prognosis of his counsellor-potential, based upon his reactions to the normal school situation and relationships.

Beyond this teacher-in-the-school analysis, evidence of activities outside the school is helpful. Voluntary youth and community service, in almost any sort of organisation, spring to mind as appropriate, but no one should be rejected at this relatively early stage solely because there is no knowledge of this. Neither should candidates be rejected because they enjoy the things that are commonly enjoyed by other people: the cinema, theatre, and music; participating in or watching sport of any kind; reading, radio, television; social activities of every sort. The last thing to be encouraged is the notion that a counsellor ought to be a dehydrated ascetic, incapable of the simpler pleasures of living, and devoid of the capacity to enjoy life as other people enjoy it and to display a keen sense of humour. Exalted intellectual interests which are so absorbing as to exclude every other sort of commoner activity are sometimes a bar to a concern for people. How a potential counsellor occupies his spare time is often a useful indication of his adaptability, resilience and breadth of interest, but not everyone can find the energy or the opportunity for community-service activities, especially those which are available during school holidays, when teachers are more readily available.

When this initial enquiry, derived from school and whatever outside sources are available, is complete, it may indeed serve to exclude from further consideration candidates who are wholly and demonstrably unsuitable, but only in such rare cases should it be regarded as a bar to further consideration of a candidate. It needs careful assessment and analysis which is as objective as possible. Who shall conduct this assessment is an extremely important question, not only to individual applicants but also to the whole business of counselling. One imperative is that it should lie in the hands of those who believe that counselling is a significant and valuable educational service, and who know something about counselling and the demands it makes upon the counsellor. Heads and others who are not in either of these positions clearly cannot make reliable judgements about counselling-potential. Indeed, to return momentarily to the reports on candidates, one cannot expect Heads who think little of the service to make dependable comments about those who apply for it, but in practice it would seem that teachers on their staffs are unlikely to be interested because of lack of encouragement. The number of applicants is only likely to grow as interest spreads among authorities, administrators and Heads. Methods of assessing these reports will also undergo refinement and sophistication in the future to enhance their objectivity, but for the present, report-analysis should most sensibly lie in the hands of a team of assessors consisting of people with three types of experience. The first group should consist of Heads or experienced senior teachers who actively favour the spread of counselling as a purposeful educational activity; the second should comprise people who have experience of counselling, either in school, if possible, or out of it; for the third, behaviour science specialists must be recruited.

The three components of this assessing team contribute opinions based upon their own specialised knowledge and view of the task. The Heads, and there should be two or three in their group, both sexes being represented, can make judgements in terms of the candidates' professional capability in the school situation. The counsellors can form opinions of the candidates in the light of their experience of the sort of people who have in the past become successful counsellors: ideally this group also should consist of two or three people, again representing both sexes, of whom at least one should be a counsellor with specific experience of personal counselling in school. It will not, I think, be sufficient for this purpose solely to have had experience of careers guidance, for example, or purely psychological testing. It may be difficult at first to find suitable people, but as teacher-counsellors become less scarce than they are now it will be easier. These two groups, the Heads and the counsellors, will be able to form opinions about the general suitability of the candidates for counselling in the school environment. The third section of this team should consist of people who are qualified to make more clinical assessments about the stability of candidates' personality. Gloucestershire Education Authority, in selecting people for EPR, stipulate an interview with a psychiatrist; Birmingham, to whom I also referred earlier, in selecting teachers for sex education do not indicate in their booklet the composition of the interviewing committee, only that there will be one. One thing seems to be essential – that laymen with no knowledge of counselling or teaching should be specifically excluded from any stage of selection for this specialised personal service. Some teachers to whom I have talked dislike intensely the prospect of an interview with a psychologist or a psychiatrist. This attitude could reflect a genuine nervousness about their ability to present themselves well in front of what they imagine will be a penetrating interview with a clinical expert, and might imply a genuine measure of self-criticism in their make-up which is to their credit. On the other hand, it could suggest that they still retain the suspicion that interviews with behaviour experts inevitably connote some degree of mental instability. No one stating their dislike of clinical interviews has ever given me a reason, other than hints of an attitude to psychological problems which was redolent of the ancient view of leprosy. Whichever way we view this attitude to a personal clinical interview on the part of a highly trained and experienced teacher, we might suspect that it suggests an inbuilt unsuitability for counselling. There is, however, no doubt in my own mind that the assessing panel must contain one, or two, psychologists or psychiatrists, whose special knowledge is a valuable contribution to the panel's assessment of a candidate's suitability. At least a behaviour specialist might be expected to rule out those candidates with personality defects recognisable to him in the light of his special experience, without subjective or professional prejudice. For those who fear that this person, who has no knowledge of school working environment, might reject or accept them solely on the grounds of a single interview, it should be remembered that at least half of the assessing team consists of people with school experience, and that decisions will be the whole team's, not a single person's! It is important that feelings of this last sort should be dispelled because the selection must not only be rigorous in itself but also fair and seen to be fair.

We have now to consider how the assessing team will arrive at its conclusions. If the foregoing recommendations about its constitution are accepted, it will consist of something between a maximum of eight and a minimum of five people with different experiences and viewpoints. This may seem expensive in personnel, but to reduce the number below five increases the element of doubt due to personal prejudice. The team could work through a series of interviews. This possibility has two objections to it. The first is that interviews are notoriously unreliable; selecting teachers for posts reveals this, and one practised interviewer of university candidates once observed that they gave undue advantage to attractive young women and well-spoken men. The second is that a succession of separate interviews with different individual assessors does not give the latter an opportunity of studying a particular candidate under the same conditions at the same time. Even the collective interview, one person being seen by a collection of selectors, is a wholly artificial procedure, and unless it is organised with exceptional care it provides only a brief snapshot of its subject under very artificial and tense conditions; it has little search or penetration value and slight relevance on its own to a search for those qualities which are needed in a counsellor. We need instead a technique of studying a candidate over a more extended period so that he can be observed by some or all of the assessing panel at the same time under conditions which highlight the qualities for which the panel is searching. I suppose that this might have to be continued indefinitely in order to be sure of the outcome. In practice, one or two days seems, if Marriage Guidance selection experience is any guide, to be a reasonable period. During this period the candidate can be continuously observed, not alone but in company with between six and ten other candidates. Their time is spent in a variety of relevant activities: these might consist largely of group discussion on topics related to the work for which they are offering themselves. Possible topics are situations of the sort that they may encounter in counselling itself, the ethics and morality of the service, its relation to their teaching work, and to other forms of school and allied social services. Notwithstanding my earlier opinions about the value of interviews, it is desirable that each candidate should be interviewed by the clinical expert(s) and by one or two of the heads as a part of the whole exercise. These interviews should be relaxed to the point of being informal conversations between interviewer and interviewee, and sufficiently long to have some analytical value, for example, in the estimate they provide of the time it takes for a given candidate to relax himself under the taxing conditions of an interview with a stranger. Moreover they will be conducted by people who are expert in this art and know what they are looking for, rather than amateurs who might be easily impressed by superficialities. Candidates should also be assessed by being asked to prepare brief appraisals of situations based on information presented to them about half an hour beforehand; they should present these appraisals to the group, and join in the ensuing discussion of their ideas. The suggestion has also been made that some experience of role-playing, that is acting out, for example, an interview between counsellor and client *ad hoc*, ought to be included. A further possible elaboration is to include some species of standardised test of intelligence and of personality.

All this intense activity constitutes what we call a selection conference, which in my view should last, residentially, for two days, starting at say nine-thirty one morning, lasting until nine the same night, starting at the same time the following morning and ending about four p.m. This is certainly an exhausting experience, even allowing for fairly generous breaks for meals and coffee: and some teachers on an EPR course, who were subjected to similar long periods of discussion intermingled with factual lecture sessions, felt that this was too much of an endurance test, that nerves and concentration were taxed to breaking point, that the procedure was altogether unrealistic and that it should have been spread over four or five days in a more diluted form instead of two and a half days of intense pressure. This was a course, not a selection conference, and it was not residential; had it been so it is possible that some of the stress might have been 'talked out' in the informal conversations which take place on residential courses when the business of the day is complete. On the other hand, other teachers on this course felt its intensity was appropriate and necessary. This group included some who in my knowledge and judgement had already formed extremely relaxed relationships with students in their school. For them the course appeared to be as much a support as a further training for the work they had already begun on their own initiative. The purpose of such an intensive selection procedure is to provoke in the candidates the

emotional and nervous reaction which can occur during counselling. We cannot really and wholly simulate, *in vacuo* as it were,
the conditions of counselling, however carefully we employ role-
playing methods in attempts to involve potential counsellors in
dramatised copies of counselling situations. There is an unavoid-
able air of artificiality about such activities, although they may
have a restricted use in selection and training. We can, however,
try to ascertain whether an intending counsellor has the emotional
and other resources to handle serenely any situation which his
prospective clients might present. Clearly it is highly desirable
that this should be found out before he begins to train for his new
work. This is what a selection conference seeks to do. It attempts
to set up conditions under which the person who is likely to lose
his temper or become irritated will do so, the person whose
opinions are fixed will display this fact about himself, those to
whom certain situations and subjects are quite intolerable and
find it difficult to conceal their intolerance will reveal themselves,
and those who remain unruffled under all circumstances will
show up favourably.

When the conference is over on the second day it then becomes
the assessing team's job to make decisions about the suitability of
the candidates as they have shown themselves during the conference and in relation to the preliminary reports which the team has
about each of them. The constitution of the selection team is such
as to reduce personal bias to a minimum and to make their
decisions about candidates' suitability as objective as is possible
within the limits imposed by current knowledge and experience
in this new field of educational practice. How the team arrives at
its decisions is for it to decide. In any given group of candidates
there are likely to be those who seem so obviously suitable as to
require little discussion; so also, the blatantly unsuitable candidates
will stand out. It is the middle-range candidates who will present
the difficulties, as they do in other forms of assessment. The
qualities which the team will be looking for, and which I have

already suggested, do not lend themselves readily to precise quantitative objective measurement. It is possible, however, to construct a rating scale for each of the appropriate qualities in a given candidate, ranging from, say, one to five, and from these to compile a set of rating totals for each candidate. Such totals may then be compared with an arbitrary score which is regarded as a bar to selection. This reeks of examinations and formal pass-fail procedures, and determining the qualifying total might present some difficulty in the light of present rather inadequate knowledge of how to assess the attributes which are sought. We may come to such a procedure in the future, but I am inclined to regard this as an unduly sophisticated way of making selection decisions which could be made with equal satisfaction through informal discussion among the assessors about the impressions and information they have concerning the candidates. When all is said and done, the authority which organises a selection conference on these lines will choose its selection panel for their skill and experience, and somewhat dubious attempts at quantification are scarcely justifiable – at least at present.

The candidates about whom there may be some doubt – the middle-range candidates referred to earlier – merit special attention in two respects. First, I do not believe that it will help the development of a counselling service to be lenient about selection. Any candidate about whose suitability there is any doubt should be rejected by the selection team. There is no benefit at all to be gained from the 'we might as well take a chance with Mr X' attitude to selection. It might in fact turn out that Mr X proved himself in practical service as a teacher-counsellor, but if, in the event, Mr X proved himself unable to cope with real crisis then the counselling service would be brought into disrepute and the selection process with it. Having established this, it is important that no decision of unsuitability should be final in the sense of prohibiting once and for all the Mr Xs of this world from teacher-counselling for ever. Every rejected candidate should be able to

apply for selection not less than one year after a selection conference which classed him as unsuitable, with a limit of three rejections. Furthermore, candidates whose rejection is borderline,
those with whom the assessing panel might have felt inclined
under less rigorous conditions to take a chance, might well be
recommended to apply in a year's time. Such a course of action
might be particularly relevant to younger candidates, whose
prospects might be materially improved at the end of a further
year's maturation and development. Preference might well be
given to such candidates when applications for subsequent selection conferences are considered. On the other hand, it would be
wise not to allow rejected people to apply at regular yearly
intervals, and it does not seem unreasonable to tell a candidate who
has been turned down by three conferences that he should not
apply again. Clearly, confidential records will have to be kept
about every candidate who offers himself, on which the assessing
panel must inscribe their view of each candidate and the particular reasons for rejecting any one. Any selection conference will
have to pay attention to such comments, and if it were to appear
that, for example, the same weakness or a related one occurred
every time a particular candidate presented himself for selection,
it would be justifiable to conclude that this represented a constant
personality factor which would be unlikely to change with the
passage of time. Allowing such a person to continue presenting
himself would waste the time of selecting panels, obstruct the entry
of a more suitable candidate, and raise unjustifiable hopes of
future success in the mind of the person concerned.

I have discussed selection procedure at some length, yet the
outline of a selection conference is incomplete and offers guide
lines rather than a specific programme, because methods of selection and training are bound to change as knowledge and experience with counselling in schools improve. But selection, in my
opinion, is at least as important as subsequent training, and may
well be more significant. If the relevant personal qualities are

lacking in candidates I doubt whether training, however intense
or professional it may be, can compensate for their absence.
Attempting to train everyone who offers himself would be extremely wasteful of time and money, and the provision that any
candidate may offer himself three times before being finally
rejected disposes, I hope, of any objections to this kind of selection
procedure which may be raised by over-enthusiastic volunteers.
It is difficult to estimate the proportion of teachers in secondary
schools who would be likely to meet with acceptance. There may
be more than we might at first suspect. For a number of teachers
work under conditions and have to abide by school customs which
effectively stifle the development of the personal qualities which
they possess and which are needed for counselling services,
qualities which might reveal themselves under different circumstances and with different opportunities. The attitudes of Heads,
governors, parents and committees are extremely influential here
and some teachers are transformed by a change of Head, authority
and régime, from the mundane to the inspired, from the oppressed
to the relaxed – and in the reverse direction. The personal qualities
are there; only the environment changes, from one which sup-
presses these qualities to one which fosters them. A good selection
conference should elicit such attributes and may indeed lead to a
view of a candidate which is at variance with the preliminary
report on him, although this should be an extremely rare occur-
rence if preliminary reports are properly compiled.

TRAINING

An earlier comment that selection is possibly more important
than training may imply that training is unnecessary. Some
teachers may indeed need very little training, others may need
much: to the former, training will be a buttress to the relaxed
and knowledgeable outlook they already have, while to the
latter it will be enlightening as well. But training there must be.
In many respects, training should be a continuation of selection

procedures, and if it is thought that this is a further daunting and exhausting prospect, it is important to remind ourselves that selection, and indeed training, while they are strenuous and searching, are intended to be conducted in a relaxed and friendly atmosphere. The tutors in both phases will certainly be at ease; any strain that exists will therefore come from the candidates themselves, and although this is only to be expected in the first session or two of both, any continuance of this unease will tend to reflect the inability of the affected candidates for the work rather than incorrect training.

Certain prime conditions must be satisfied by any form of training. It must be relevant, and seen to be so; it must comprise an initial course, the duration of which we shall discuss later; and there must be continued in-service training under supervision, during which teacher-counsellors meet and discuss cases and experiences under experienced leadership. This last is an imperative for any counselling service and its training system, for few things are more damaging to a counsellor, his work, or his image, than the feeling or belief that he is isolated or omniscient, both of which can be corrected by continued in-service training, case discussion and competent supervision.

There are two current forms of initial training in counselling or cognate subjects available in this country. Certain colleges of education provide optional courses in youth-leadership, careers guidance, and social work, and students can elect to pursue whichever is available. The aims seems to be to equip them to deal with careers selection problems, to handle young people in a pupil-centred rather than a subject-centred way, and to undertake social welfare duties. While these activities can easily spill over into something like personal counselling, they are not identical with it. Moreover, since this form of training is directed at student-teachers in initial training it is not particularly relevant to training experienced teachers who are interested in counselling; and I have already urged objections in principle to the incorporation of counselling or guidance training in a young teacher's first course in college. For these reasons, and these alone, no purpose is served by discussing this further in these pages.

The Universities of Manchester, Keele and Reading provide diploma courses, lasting one year on a full-time basis. Other universities have similar projects under development. These courses are highly professional. They vary slightly from one establishment to another in approach and emphasis but they all contain elements of counselling and guidance which are closely related to some of the problems I have encountered in personal counselling. However, the full-time one-year course appears to have as its aim the production of a highly trained specialist rather than a teacher-counsellor. This may not in fact be the deliberate intention of the course organisers but its extremely comprehensive nature rather implies that its products can scarcely justify the time, money and expertise expended on them in anything other than full-time counselling posts in schools or in supporting educational services such as child guidance. With variations in detail from one university to another these courses cover in considerable depth educational psychology, educational measurement and testing, child development, the theory and practice of guidance and counselling, educational administration, environmental influences and change in relation to education and other cognate topics. Moreover, similar items appear under different titles in the courses offered by different establishments: a useful summary appears in *Working Paper No. 15* of the Schools Council. Much emphasis is laid on sociometric and psychometric methods, statistics, attitudes and interests. Such courses seem therefore to be geared to professional and objective expertise in the total field of child guidance, of which counselling in the personal sense is merely one part. While I would not question the motives of the course organisers, it seems to me that the emergence of yet another category of educational expert upon whose broad and omniscient shoulders almost every school difficulty might well be unloaded, is not the most pertinent solution to the kind of personal problem with which I am concerned and to which the answers on an objective test sheet may contribute little in the form of help which is appreciated by the client, however much this species of counsellor may so learn about him. Clinical objectivity is not the same as a caring relationship: the former is implicitly impersonal, the latter never is. On a broader issue, I still rather doubt whether our knowledge of the development of human personality is adequate enough to allow us to approach the problems of day-to-day human feelings and actions in anything other than a mood of total humility and care, for which plain expertise is a poor substitute. Thus, a one-year full-time course is not, as I see it, the most appropriate form of training for teacher-counsellors, simply because it seeks to train a different sort of person from a teacher-counsellor. We can dismiss it for present purposes for this reason alone, apart from consideration of money or the withdrawal of scarce and experienced teachers from their schools for a whole year. I do not expect a personal teacher-counsellor to be able to include among his duties careers advice, psychological testing, interviews with parents in school about curriculum problems, keeping detailed personal records, clinical assistance to teachers on the staff, assessment of abilities, interests, attitudes and achievements, child-motivation, home visiting, to mention some of the duties which the *Working Paper* lists as being undertaken by school counsellors. There are plenty of competent teachers who can cope with one or more of these, although not all. Specifically I expect a personal counsellor to know where he can obtain further specialised advice or help in school or outside it which might come under one or other of these headings and which are beyond his particular brief. His task is to accept his clients, and the duality of his role as a client's confidant and a member of the teaching staff.

The problem of training teacher-counsellors thus remains. Its solution seems to me to lie in a totally different approach: that of an intensive short course, post-course in-service training and follow-up refresher course, all backed by prescribed reading. Two considerations are pertinent here. The first is that short courses lasting from two days to two weeks, for example, are frequently used to bring teachers up to date in the specialist subjects. Courses and conferences arranged to familiarise teachers with the new methods and subject matter of the Nuffield Schemes exemplify this. From time to time, certain universities arrange part-time refresher courses, extending over a year or more, including one or two evening sessions per week and certain vacation periods, to bring teachers whose qualifications have become out of date into contact with new ideas and concepts in their subjects; others arrange courses involving one night per week for six to eight weeks to stimulate and reorientate teacher-thinking about instructional method and curriculum content in one specialism or another. There is thus nothing new about the conception of part-time in-service training for teachers of some experience, to reinvigorate them without losing their teaching services for long periods. There seems no good reason why similar methods should not be used to help teachers to rethink personal relationships with pupils inside their schools, instead of their teaching methods, for it is such a rethinking of relationships that is the core of training for personal counselling. There is one significant difference between subject and relational reappraisal: the latter requires preliminary selection on the lines already suggested, the former does not.

The second consideration is that some experience has already been gained with short courses which attempt such relational reorientation with selected teachers. I refer here to courses in Education in Personal Relationships (EPR) of which the Gloucestershire scheme is a classic example which is being followed in principle, if not in detail, by other local education authorities in various parts of the country. EPR is certainly not identical with personal counselling, but EPR and counselling exact from their practitioners two qualities common to both: the ability to work through and live with a relationship between students and selected members of the staff which is confidential, and the capacity to sustain a co-operative rather than an authoritarian atmosphere. Training for EPR therefore entails a reorientation of the teacher's ideas about his relationships with students, just as training for counselling does; and if the one can be accomplished on a short-course, part-time basis, there seems no good reason why a similar approach should not be attempted for the other. It does not necessarily follow that a teacher who can cope easily with the group methods of EPR can face as equably the more intimate problems of personal counselling; neither would the reverse be necessarily true. Group discussion teaching as an organised part of the time-table and covering a fairly standard set of topics, despite its informality and non-authoritarian context, is vastly different from the sometimes analytical and always peculiarly individual situations which personal counselling presents us with. The difference in depth of involvement and in operating context is almost sufficient to constitute a difference of quality rather than of degree between the two activities despite the fact that EPR does create counselling situations. It is important that teachers who are interested in these sorts of personal relationships should understand this difference, in view of the confusion which I have heard them express, and their readiness to identify the two activities which arises from this confusion. It is furthermore possible that somewhat different personality traits are required for two different kinds of involvement, although there seems no reason why suitable teachers should not essay both forms of activity provided that they undergo the relevant types of training.

What then might be included in a personal counselling course? The prerequisite, after selection, is some preliminary reading, and I suggest some relevant titles at Appendix I. The course itself could include a variety of topics and the following list, while it does not constitute an exhaustive and detailed scheme or a most suitable sequence, is a useful summary of subjects which seem to be relevant.

1. The nature of personal counselling;
2. The social background to the strains and difficulties of adolescence;
3. Adolescent development (two sessions):
   a. Physiological,
   b. Psychological;
4. The nature of teacher-student relationships;
5. Communication and feed-back in counselling;
6. External supporting agencies;
7. The teacher-counsellor's problems (three sessions):
   a. In relation to his teaching,
   b. In relation to his colleagues,
   c. In relation to parents.

These comprise what might be called the instructional themes, each of which will require an introductory talk by one or other of the tutors on the training panel. The lengths of these introductions are likely to vary with the subject, although each should be directed to stimulating thought rather than conveying information alone. The first three or four might well be, for example, three-quarters of an hour in length; the last three might well be shorter. Each talk needs to be followed up, with or without an intervening break, by discussion among the trainees of the issues raised in the talk. For such discussions the trainees should be divided into groups not exceeding ten in number and led by one of the training panel. All this accounts for twenty sessions of an instructional nature or of discussion related directly to the talks.

Trainees must also have the opportunity of 'case discussion' periods, in the same small groups under tutor leadership: that is, sessions specifically directed to considering ways of handling actual or contrived situations and problems. The intricacies of relations with colleagues and parents should be included in these as well as students' cases. One way of stimulating this is to present each trainee with a specific problem; give him, say, half an hour's notice, as in the selection conference, and ask him to outline before the other members of his discussion group how he would deal with it. His group can then discuss the problem using his proposals as a starting point. Another device is to invite two members of a group to act out a case – they can be given a short brief beforehand to help – and let their colleagues talk about their treatment. This second method is only really effective, in my view, when the two volunteers are fairly competent improvisers and reasonably capable actors, and it is not a technique of training in which anyone should be compelled to join. Case and problem discussion ought to occupy about ten more sessions.

Thus we now have a total of some thirty sessions in the course, which must thus last a minimum of six days, allocating two sessions to each morning between nine o'clock and twelve-thirty, two each afternoon between two and six o'clock, and a single session in the evening. The morning and afternoon sessions should be broken by a half-hour interval for appropriate refreshment. Such a course has to be residential: partly for reasons of time and partly because this helps to create an *esprit de corps* which grows out of the discussions which invariably continue after the day's programme is over. A relaxed atmosphere supervenes in which everyone gets to know everyone else well.

I envisage the possibility of some thirty or forty teachers being trained in this way with a staff of, say, five tutors, who between them could cover not only the specialist introductory talks but also lead the discussion groups. It may, however, be more convenient in some cases, in view of the difficulty of finding suitable residential accommodation, to take in a smaller number at a single course, using two or three tutors, and bringing in one or two outside specialists to give particular introductory talks. This is a less efficient way of employing tutor and specialist time, but the

M

balance of cost and efficiency is a delicate one which will require adjustment in particular areas. It would probably be helpful to use for the training panel some of those who comprised the selection panel for the particular group of trainees, and the convenor of the selection conference might well be the chief tutor of the course.

This is, on the face of things, a strenuous course. The fact that at least two-thirds of it consists of discussion activity possibly implies a lack of directiveness. However, no amount of formal lecturing, didactic theorising, or indeed profound reading can help a counsellor in many of the cases that come before him. It is his attitude and ability to help his client express himself clearly which matter most. The largely discursive approach to a counselling course aids him in developing these attributes, which selection has shown him to possess in some degree. Counselling, it must be reiterated, is about people and their relationships, about the constant state of flux in which they so often are, their conditions of unpredictable change about which no one can talk with much certainty. One cannot instruct people in the ways of handling other people's inter-personal amities and antagonisms and the feelings of joy and hurt which they produce. There is a mistaken view, widely held, and indeed in quarters where people should know better, that counselling can be 'taught' by, say, a dozen directive lectures, as if the total condition of people's miseries and pleasures could be encompassed by the dispassionate utterance of what is tantamount to a set of instructions. I called these training proposals a 'course'. 'Training conference' would be a better title, for it is a conferring, a sharing of views, a gradual coming to the understanding of other people's emotions and attitudes by experiencing together the varied attitudes and outlooks of the trainees: it is an acclimatisation to new relationships. Of course there is some basis of factual knowledge, especially in the field of adolescent development, which has to be imparted to those who quite probably lack it, but this again is simply a springboard for discussing the issues which arise from it, as an aid to understanding the special problems which may confront those who counsel the young.

One omission may seem strange. I have so far made no specific reference to the sexual problems of adolescents. This is not because they do not arise in youth-counselling; of course they do and they require the same imperturbable handling as other problems. It is rather because phenomena of sexual development and activity among adolescents are better treated as part of the development and behaviour of the whole person, instead of a biological function meriting specific emphasis. Not everyone will agree with this, and it may be wise to increase the two talks on development so as to give particular attention to this matter. My view, however, is that the sessions devoted to the physiological and psychological aspects of adolescence are bound to pay considerable attention to sexual matters, and that discussion periods devoted to these two topics, as well as case-work, must include some sexual problems and difficulties. These can be seen as part of the total life and activity of the clients who raise them, rather than topics which are isolated, or unconnected with other kinds of problems and difficulties. Fluent generalisations of this kind, however, scarcely satisfy those who see the sexual relationship as something more than a merely animal act of reproduction, and regard it as the final compelling act of love between two people on the highest possible plane of human relationships. Disseminating sexual fact does not of itself help to this conclusion, neither is it a substitute for understanding the feelings which follow in the wake of sexual growth or the turbulent effect it has upon adolescent relationships, not only with contemporaries of the opposite sex but with everyone else, and parents in particular. Adolescents are not greatly inclined to accept conventional restrictions on sexual behaviour without good and cogent reasons, and the facts of venereal disease and birth control may help to some extent here. Yet I suspect that large numbers of adolescents who indulge in sexual experiment do not, in the emotions of the moment, use contraceptive preparations, and probably think that VD always happens to someone else, not them. We are therefore forced back on a discursive counselling approach to the problem, in which responsibility and consideration for the other party's individuality are really the issues at stake. Each young person will make up his own mind about his line of conduct, and for a counsellor to deal with a sexual problem by postulating predetermined rules at the outset is to invite in his client the decision to press on with what he intended to do anyway, simply as a gesture of defiant independence. By contrast with this approach I recall inviting some thirty youth-leaders to break up into groups at a conference and discuss their attitudes to sexual relationships. Nearly an hour later the conference reassembled and the four leaders of the groups stood up one after another and asked for my views. I gave them, prefacing them with the statement: 'You asked for my views; they were not forced upon you. Whether you take any notice of them is for you to settle according to whether you think they have any value. Of one thing I am certain and that is that you will not act upon them simply because a much older person has given them. You will weigh them carefully, and make your own moral decisions.' This is the essence of the counselling approach to a problem which concerns large numbers of people, perhaps unduly. Because the counsellor can listen to a youthful client and accords him dignity and responsibility, he is much more likely than not to elicit the same appreciation from his client of other people's individuality and dignity. Counselling in sexual problems is therefore no different in principle and practice from that in others. Training programmes cannot, and should not, attempt to exclude it deliberately, but to devote large parts of a course simply to this facet of the whole human being is a distortion.

Any counsellor who believes that a short conference of this type, or a longer and more formal course, is the end of the matter, is seriously mistaken. No one can hope, or should expect, to become the complete counsellor after a course of any duration, or even years of experience. He needs continuous training and self-criticism while he is doing the work; he must have the opportunity of discussing his own experiences with other counsellors, and learning from them, as they will learn from him, how to improve and develop his attitudes and insight. It is obviously impossible for one person to do this by himself. Thus, three months after his first training conference, for example, it should be obligatory for every counsellor to meet, for a one-day conference, those who were his colleagues on the conference under the leadership of one or two of their tutors, to assess their experience, discuss their results – in so far as they have any – and study their feelings, frustrations and disappointments up to that point. Learning by experience is one thing; assessing it critically is another, and counselling by other counsellors in a group under competent leadership is currently the best way of accomplishing this. And not only a single in-service training conference is needed, but regular ones, at least once a year. Beyond this guided continuous training there is a great need for regular meetings of counsellors, say once a month, for an evening's discussion of day-to-day problems, in informal surroundings also under leadership. Moreover, this should not be looked upon as a pleasant option, but as part of the counsellor's whole training programme, a mandatory part of his activity without which he cannot do his job as a counsellor properly, or maintain the trust and confidence, not only of his clients, but also of his colleagues and others associated with his school. An added benefit is that regular meetings of this kind give a counsellor the opportunity of some tutorial guidance, or reassurance. This is important, because the nature of counselling and the records which a counsellor keeps are not such as to permit the kind of inspectorial activity that is possible with conventional school subjects where there are teaching schemes to be perused and written work to be studied. The prospect of peripatetic inspectors coming into schools and asking teacher-counsellors for half a dozen cases to inspect depresses me. Counsellors need to know where their tutors can be found if necessary so that they can call on their services as they can call on other specialist agencies when occasion demands. More benefit is derivable from two counsellors in a school talking about their cases in private than a sophisticated inquisitorial machine.

Regular meetings, too, can show whether a teacher-counsellor is 'cracking' under the strain, whether of counselling itself, or the conflicts of his dual role. If his tutors feel that this is happening he should be advised to give it up for a short period, and let his headmaster know quietly without undue fuss. There is nothing inherently damaging in this, and Heads who have any under-standing at all of the stresses of counselling will see the wisdom of such a course. This benefits the image of the counselling service by highlighting the care devoted to superintendence of its prac-titioners. The same good will also accrue if, during the first train-ing course, the tutors notice that one or two already selected candidates are not surviving the strain very well, and suggest that the people concerned should return to a later course before they start counselling. Counsellors are human beings and subject to the same private stresses as other people: ill-health in his family, even a common cold of his own, other domestic worries can all reduce his effectiveness considerably, if only temporarily. It is a wise counsellor who recognises the inadequacies, however short-lived, of his work and the reasons for it, and seeks temporary respite from a most exacting duty through his tutor.

Part-time training courses can be criticised on the grounds of superficiality and ineffectiveness, although I have rarely heard this argument urged against the use of such a procedure in improving teachers' subject knowledge. The essential criterion is not the length of time devoted to the course, but the seriousness with which the course is treated by tutors and trainees, and how effec-tive are the follow-up and supervision which succeed it. More-over, trainee counsellors are not only teachers who are reasonably well educated people, but also volunteers for the work, who have been selected for the personal qualities which are appropriate to it. They are not people starting from scratch; they are already partly adapted, mentally and temperamentally, for a new kind of educational activity; they have begun the modification of attitude which counselling requires in their own minds already. Thus a part-time system of training seems to offer some possibilities, to put it no higher. It has been suggested to me that the training could be equally well accomplished by a series of evenings, for example, one night per week for fifteen weeks. This has only one merit – economy – and it is largely based upon the totally false assumption that a succession of lectures by experts will be sufficient. Yet even if we replace these by a programme of discussions, the purpose of training is not fulfilled. There is no continuity about a training schedule each session of which is separated from the preceding one by a time gap of one week. Time is wasted in recapitulation because trainees partly forget what happened the previous week; the course becomes a sort of information market, not a training in techniques and attitudes. However much the word 'conditioning' has acquired unpleasant connotations, a course in counselling is basically a self-conditioning process, not an imparting of data. This being so, a week's gap between sessions almost completely vitiates the nature and purpose of the training, because it gives trainees time to recover from the pressures which the sessions impose upon them, and opportunity for the newly discovered habits of counselling to be obliterated by the routine procedures of normal teaching. A residential week immerses the trainees in a continuous counselling atmosphere, so that it is easy for them to relate the content and debate of one session to that of another. Their feelings and inhibitions, doubts and uncertainties, are taxed and revealed respectively to the point at which they express what they really think. They can continue argument into the small hours, if necessary, until they are fully attuned to the strains and stresses which counselling creates.

Each session can start where the last ended if need be; and the week's programme should be somewhat adaptable to allow this. There is no need to recapitulate, as there is in periods separated by weeks, what was said before in order to establish continuity, for they have no time in which to forget.

Thus, a short intensive residential course, of about a week's duration, under capable leadership, followed by regular one-day conferences, supported by at least monthly discussions, with the availability of tutors for reference in times of difficulty, and backed up by the knowledge and skills of specialist social agencies, offers a possible way of training teachers in the arts of personal counselling. It does not withdraw teachers from their schools for long periods; it does not, in purely financial terms, approach the cost of taking a single teacher out of his school for a year. All the parts of this scheme are essential; I have little doubt that difficulties can be raised, but difficulties will always argue most cogently for themselves. If, as I believe, personal counselling in schools is a necessary educational service, means will be found to overcome them and whether selection and training for teacher-counsellors takes the form recommended in this chapter or not, selection and training there must be.

SUMMARY

Certain qualities are required of a personal teacher-counsellor. These cannot be inculcated; they need to be there, concealed perhaps but nonetheless real. Therefore a selection procedure is needed. Selection presents certain professional problems, concerning professional status and advancement, which are however irrelevant to the outlook and function of a teacher-counsellor. Selection needs to be rigorous as a step towards a new form of professional involvement. Certain desiderata of age, professional experience and competence need to be observed, but these are not specifically intellectual or academic. The final arbiter of suitability should be a residential selection conference lasting two days in which candidates are assessed by a team consisting of senior teachers, counsellors and psychologists or psychiatrists. The training recommended for the specific purposes of personal counselling, as distinct from products of one-year diploma courses intended to meet the demands in much wider fields of guidance, is a one-week residential course of an intensive nature, followed by further in-service training and support. This is largely discursive, although there is an element of didactic instruction. Training is never complete; it must be continuous. Lectures are irrelevant and inadequate, unless as a basis for discussion, and even then must be sparsely used. Training is absolutely essential.

VI. Moral Aspects of Counselling

Although I have touched on the moral implications of the counsellor's position in Chapter II, no treatment of counselling can justifiably omit some further consideration of whatever moral principles underlie the activity. Such principles as there may be not only govern, consciously or otherwise, a counsellor's approach to his work, but also pervade, intangibly perhaps, the atmosphere of the counselling room. At secondhand, as it were, they are the oil upon the troubled waters of the client's condition. It is also imperative that we understand as much as we possibly can, and in the least complicated manner, about the ethos of a service which may affect, perhaps very profoundly, the lives of other and younger people, some of them at a crucial stage of their personal development. Any suggestion of certainty or arrogance in the following pages is wholly unintended, and I do not pretend to offer firm conclusions: but to discuss the moral issues even briefly, even with some degree of confused superficiality, may help those who contemplate counselling as part of their educational service, by stimulating their own thoughts about motives and attitudes as well as about the moral aspects of the matter.

To begin with – and it is the only valid starting point – let us examine the counselling relationship and make certain assumptions which appear to be valid in the light of what has gone before in this book. If you, the reader, are the client and I am the counsellor, what passes between us is unique and not wholly communicable to anyone else. It is unique because there are most probably no two other people who are identical with – not just similar to – us in existence and if there were the probability of their meeting and making a relationship under circumstances identical with ours is infinitesimal. It is not completely communicable to anyone else not because counselling stipulates that it must not be communicated, but because it cannot be described to anyone else in terms which a third person can wholly understand. It is a unique, unidentical experience. The joint excursion through counselling concerns and involves no one else directly. Its success, in whatever terms – if any are available for its estimation – depends upon the creation of a relationship which has its own individual nature and stretches across the differences between us. If we think about it more carefully than we have done so far we will find that this relationship discounts differences of articulateness and literacy, of dialect and idiom, of attitude and manner, of appearance and attire, of age and generation, of outlook and values, of conduct and belief. We accept each other in the end absolutely as we are. The experience is not affected by the subtle shades of meaning which words and phrases assume according to the circumstances and tone of their utterance; neither party infers from what is said interpretations which are not intended, but both seek whatever clarification seems necessary to them so that any trace of ambiguity and doubt is minimised. It disregards the mistakes which both make and the relationship grows from a persistent attempt at mutual communication which both parties to it know and implicitly agree can never be complete or absolute because each is a discrete individual. It also depends, and I believe this to be the core of the matter, upon a recognition by each other of the other's personal existence and value, neither of which in the present state of our knowledge is quantifiable: and by quantifiable I mean capable of expression in the precise and definitive terms of the mathematician or the physical scientist. For this assessment of what passes between client and counsellor is far removed from the cool and impersonal objectivity of the scientist analysing what comes out of his test tubes or recording what happens to his instruments. It is infinitely more complex than the ramifications of the behaviour of molecules, atoms, electrons and other particles, once so esoteric, but now quite well understood.

If we look at less sophisticated and more everyday examples of relationships between simple material, the contrast with the counselling relationship is even plainer. We know what will happen if we put a teaspoonful of a common brand of liver salts into water, when we add some detergent to a bowl full of greasy plates, or a lighted match to a gas jet. The more involved mixtures which are the staple of pastry- and cake-making are almost as predictable in behaviour. Our whole domestic life is largely governed nowadays by knowledge of this kind which enables us to foretell what will happen when we perform certain common actions. No questions of human trust or judgement are involved. We are using relationships between substances, the rules governing which have been elucidated over the years by patient experiment and calculation, with increasing refinement: we are dealing with clear and comprehensible facts, some of which we may ultimately disregard at our peril, and many of which are the background to the day-to-day instructions which appear on the sides of packages of health salts, detergents, cake and pastry mixtures or medicines. By contrast relationships between people are incredibly complicated and unpredictable.

If, however, we look again at the relationship between us there are, without doubt, certain facts to be observed by each of us about the other which, for reasons we do not need to investigate here, provoke reactions in both of us, reactions which range from the hostile to the friendly. These are the external and superficial criteria of height and weight, of face and expression, of dress and bearing, of speech and demeanour, all of them stimuli in each of us for responses in the other, and neither may care much about why. In any case these are rather trivial matters, and the initial reactions to them will almost certainly pass as we talk and the relationship grows. But, as we talk – and you will talk more – other facts emerge, more about you than about me, since your facts are the relevant and important ones in this counselling journey. These are deeper and more important, and they comprise what we rather learnedly call the sociological data: where you live, how many there are in your family, your position in it, what your living accommodation is really like, the family income, the educational background of everyone in it, the family's health record. On this sort of information sociologists can construct hypotheses about your attitudes and behaviour and make some prognostications about relevant action, which may have some validity. But this personal-physical and family-social information, while it may be complete in itself, gives nonetheless an incomplete picture of you for it leaves out how you feel about these facts: whether you are angry, happy, anxious, relaxed, frustrated, content, miserable, or whatever other emotional reactions you have to them. It is how you feel about them that interests me as a counsellor as much as, if not more than, the facts themselves. After this, it is my task as a counsellor to try to find out why you feel the way you do. And if this can be elicited, helping you to understand why you feel the way you do becomes a possibility. Finally, when we have come to some understanding of why you feel the way you do feel about the facts of your situation, we can begin to come to terms with it, or think about what you can do about it – if anything can be done. Thus, the facts and the feelings together are the start of producing, on your part, a plan for action, or an ability to co-exist with a situation about which, for the moment at least, you may be able to do nothing, apart perhaps from achieving some peace of mind, and living with circumstances which, according to your case, may vary from the merely trying to the extremely tragic.

I have recapitulated the growth of my counsellor's relationship with you, my client, to educe two special features. The first is that the relationship contained elements which were scientific-objective because they were based on ascertainable facts about you, and elements which were non-scientific-subjective because they were

based upon your feelings. Both these components of the relationship were significant. Which was more so was very much a
matter of opinion, but neither of them could be neglected by me
nor any counsellor at any level. The second facet of the relationship
was what I, the counsellor, did. In essence I did nothing, in what
was nonetheless a rather involved operation; I, and you, gave up
some time. I provided patience, interest, sympathy, a willing ear,
a few comments and questions to stimulate your thinking, and a
rather small amount of specialised knowledge. I shall return later
to the dichotomy in the counselling relationship, and to the
possible moral significance of the counsellor's contribution as I
have just described it. For the moment I want to break off and
look briefly at a teacher's possible view of this, and deal with one
or two particular questions about caring.

But why go to all this trouble, it may be asked. For adults in
difficulty possibly, but not for volatile teenagers, happy one
moment, depressed the next, angry at half past three, joyful at
four. It is, of course, very easy to credit one's self with high-
sounding motives, which counsellors, as we shall see, are not very
eager to do, but it seems to me that there is only one reason for
taking the kind of trouble which is entailed in the counselling
process. This reason is that other people matter; because they exist
they are important, significant, valuable – use any epithet you
like, and give it as much meaning or weight as you care to ascribe
to it. Yet many teachers will surely argue that all their pupils
matter to them. Why then this implication of a distinction between the moral attitude of the counsellor and that of the non-
counsellor?

The answer, as I see it, is something like this. My special subject
is Chemistry. Some students love it, some tolerate it, others detest
it. They have also a similar range of attitudes to me as a person;
and some critical essays written by students about me are a serious
and searchingly lucid challenge to any teacher's complacency – I
commend this exercise to any teacher who feels pleased with him-

self or is thinking of taking up counselling. If any student of mine performs badly in Chemistry tests I see little purpose in publicly haranguing him – there may be much to be said for speaking to him privately – for, as Dietrich Bonhoeffer observed, to abuse a person is to destroy him or to strip him of his dignity. If he belongs to one of the groups that do not hate the subject I can tell him privately what the consequences might be in terms of information to parents, recommendations to future employers and general merit-worthiness. This puts a burden of responsible decision upon his shoulders, and, perhaps for the first time, he has to blame himself for failure, not someone else. If he hates the subject, I tell him that we cannot arrange for him to do something else instead because we have not the space or staff to manage this. These are facts of life, which are inescapable in the given school context, and I help him to accept them responsibly. In both cases students are helped in the subject sense towards self-control and responsibility. Of course, this may be easier than it sounds, and some readers may conclude that I am negligent in my duty, or taking an easy way out. Let me remind them, however, that it is much easier to bellow like an angry bull at some test-failing youth, or berate a lad who has not done his homework, than it is to find out why this happens, whatever it is, to make him believe that I think he has some virtue behind his sullenness and non-co-operation, and lead him to self-respect and responsibility, using formal teacher's sanctions only as a last resort. This is not to say that I see no value in my subject, or in any other for that matter: of course I do, but I regard the acquisition of a sense of responsibility, or a start along the road to it, as a far more significant achievement than learning the structure of a crystal of common salt. There are nowadays no absolute unchallengeable sanctions which compel students to learn. What matters now is not the facts which are learned but the acquisition of a sense of responsibility. The distinction between teacher and teacher-counsellor is that the former cares about his students because they have not learned their facts and about his own contractual duty to see that they learn them, while the latter cares when his students have not begun to behave responsibly. These two forms of caring are not the same at all, and I believe that to achieve a sense of responsibility in an adolescent is not only a performance of greater intrinsic moral worth but is also, in conventional school terms, a very profitable accomplishment because it leads to improved work, better results and superior behaviour.

To return to our counselling relationship – apart from a purely intellectual satisfaction at understanding something well, it does not matter much to me what the counselling process really entails apart from the personal relationship itself. We can certainly discern objective-scientific elements in it because we have to consider the sort of hard facts about clients to which I have already referred, and infer tentative conclusions about possible action from them. Whether these conclusions are acceptable to him or not depends upon the highly subjective and unscientific feeling which he has about himself and the facts about him. If we pay too much attention to the facts alone, we forget his feelings; we may even make his feelings more intense and complicated by doing this, simply because he dislikes intensely, for example, his family background, and to suggest in any way that he should not feel this way only makes him think the worse of it. Yet if we forget the facts and concentrate upon his feelings we may only encourage him to live in a miasma of self-pity, to turn away from the facts instead of helping him to face them. A counsellor has to balance his treatment of this duality about the counselling relationship, and his approach to a client, simply in terms of his own judgement and attitude.

And this brings me to a fundamental conception about the counsellor's activity – that he uses relational therapy, where other fields of constructive treatment use physiotherapy, or occupational therapy and the rest. By relational therapy, I mean the express use of himself as a person, as a therapeutic agent; not the information he may supply or the opinions he may be ultimately asked to express, but the qualities which he brings to the task as a person. His patience, interest, sympathy and the other attributes he displays help his client to 'get better' simply because he displays them. Collectively, and in some inexplicable way, they influence his judgement of the best way to help his client to what I call social health. This, in a nutshell, is his purpose in counselling.

By social health I understand the ability to cope with life as it is, and to avoid those situations which experience, both everyday and clinical, suggests will bring with them continuous or intermittent wretchedness and unhappiness. I am well aware that this involves us in considering what we may mean by unhappiness and wretchedness and how far the structure and conventions of society create meanings of these terms which are not absolute but are relative to social custom. But it seems to me that I must accept the absolute indefinability of these words because I am concerned primarily here with adolescents, and my experience suggests that most of them are worried about how they can find the resources to avoid what seem to them to be prospects of misery in society as it is and that they are envious of those who are capable of doing this themselves. In parenthesis, I believe this to be true of many adults too. Moreover the young men I have met in informal discussion groups in prison seemed, as far as the majority were concerned, to be worried about their own lack of ability to avoid actions and circumstances which, even in their knowledge of life, seemed likely to bring this unhappiness upon them. Behind their bravado lay a real fear of the inability to manage their lives in such a way as to achieve the contentment in life which other people enjoyed, which they had never attained and seemed unlikely to attain. In this sense these young men were socially ill: some of them may have been mentally or physically ill also, but these states are outside the limits of my particular brief, namely social health.

What I now suggest is that the counsellor's purpose, of restoring his clients to social health, despite his total acceptance of them

N

and his express wish not to impose upon them opinions about and solutions to their problems, is a moral purpose; that the very act of concerning himself so much with his clients is a moral act, and that the subjective attributes of his own personality which are employed to help the client back to social health are moral qualities. The relative objectivity of this, the counsellor's purpose, and the sociological facts about the client, the emotional climate of the interviews, especially the first one, and the client's subjective feelings about the facts of his case, which together appear to be ambivalent or paradoxical aspects of the relationship between counsellor and client, are in fact inseparable, if distinguishable, components both of the goal at which the counsellor aims and how he moves towards it.

This duality of the scientific and the non-scientific, of the objective and the subjective in the counselling process in fact vanishes in a unity which is expressed in the moral purpose behind it. Caring, patience, sympathy used so as to restore a client to some degree of social health are moral instruments.

The word moral, of course, lands us in all sorts of difficulties, because it is used more often than not to suggest adherence to a particular set of rules, or the adoption of a recognisable collection of attitudes. In particular, these might lead many teachers to condemn out of hand the circumstances and proposals of the first case in Chapter I. Only that which is moral is contained in the rules. Acceptance of what is not within the rules is immoral, and rejection of it is moral. Such rigidity, however, throws care, sympathy, interest, patience, forbearance, and the other qualities which counsellors must display and use, out of court immediately, because they imply an acceptance of what we can call immoral frailties in others. The ethical view one takes of counselling therefore depends entirely upon our judgement of whether such qualities are moral in whatever context they are used, or whether to be moral is simply to abide by the rigid rules of the social game regardless of the condition of the client. I find it difficult to believe that human pain, misery, and squalor are anything other than what they are to anyone who cares and deliberately seeks to find out everything he can about these social ailments in another person. And pain and misery, even if they were transitory states, were evident enough in those cases I have described earlier. These maladies are not curable by a straight dose of moral rejection or apocalyptic condemnation, which only foster diseases which are already thriving strongly. The real antidotes are the qualities which a counsellor must be able to provide. The fact that in his private life he adheres to a particular set of rules need not prevent him from providing the antidotes, so long as he puts the moral worth of sympathy, patience and understanding above that of the particular moral code to which he subscribes. Here it is interesting to note that the majority of counsellors I have met have been committed members of one religious – not necessarily Christian – communion or another, but this does not prevent them from helping, in the counselling sense, clients whose activities transgressed, for example, the principles of sexual conduct in which they themselves believed. This commitment is not, however, a prerequisite of good counselling, although some basis of personal faith seems to me to be extremely sustaining to a counsellor who is faced with difficult moral problems in his clients, because it gives him a secure base from which his counselling can operate.

By all means let us be as scientific as we possibly can about whatever the client presents to us; let us examine all the facts of the case, the information which is as unassailable, say, as the death of a young man's father. But added to these facts, although less precisely definable, are his feelings about the original material ones. We must be severely critical about what information is relevant and what is not, in the way that a scientist examines his data with studied care. On the other hand a rigid scientific view of a client may easily degenerate into arrogance and impatience, and cause neglect of his feelings. A totally detached impersonal attitude eliminates any consideration of the impact of the counsellor's qualities as well as his appreciation of the sheer value of the client because he exists, which are the moral elements in the counselling relationship. Moreover it overlooks the possibility that the mere fact of the counsellor being there can influence the client, not because he instructs or directs the client in any way. There is an implication here which could affect the whole notion of totally non-directive counselling; and this is that, because a counsellor provides the time, the care and the sympathy, something of his inner self, his own set of moral attitudes, must rub off on to the client, whether he explicitly states them or not, simply because his relationship with the client implies these moral attitudes, of which a client must, at least over some period of time, become aware. Whether this is so or not, the client it is who makes the decisions, receives the moral impulses, or whatever the influences operating may be; it is not the counsellor who deliberately and intentionally transmits them.

If a counsellor is asked, as we have seen may happen, for opinions or decisions, these are acceptable and sought by his client not because he believes his counsellor's information by purely objective-scientific standards is necessarily complete, as it will not be anyway, but because his moral attitude to his client makes them acceptable. They are given by a counsellor, not because he seeks to bolster his own self-esteem, thinks he is a better person or has a desire to do good to someone, but simply as a moral act. His part is self-denying precisely because he does not play his part for these reasons, because he does not seek to make his clients dependent upon him, because he does not want to feel the client's hurt anger, sadness and anxiety for him. His version of morality helps him to understand why his client feels the way he does, even if, by objective-scientific criteria, these feelings may be irrational. And having come to understanding, by developing the relationship through his own moral qualities he begins to lead the client back to the beginnings of human rationality, back to what I have called social health. Of course a counsellor may see what he might like to call an improvement in his client: he may see a taut and strained expression slowly relax into ease, words come more coherently, humour begin to show through an oppressive atmosphere of anxiety, and his client begin to make his own suggestions about relevant action and attitude. He may see, in a school, improvement in behaviour, attitude, work and social relationships. But all these are themselves highly subjective criteria in that they represent what the assessors of such improvement may wish to see rather than what is essentially beneficial to the client. The accomplishment of this species of end-product to counselling satisfies the urge in all of us to 'do something' about an unhappy situation; and by comparison with the usual scholastic functions of school-teachers, a counsellor 'does' nothing deliberately, at least for some time. It is the mechanism, the way in which he nurses the relationship, which makes counselling meaningful and therapeutic, not to him but to his client. The sociological data which the client can provide about himself may not seem very significant to him although it may be very relevant in the counsellor's eyes to any future solution of his client's problem. On the other hand the relationship with his counsellor is significant to a client because it is a source of stability to him, because it is his alone and belongs to no one else. It is this relationship which enables a client to say something like this to himself: 'I like this chap; he is interested in me and about my situation; because he is interested and thinks some sensible outcome is possible, perhaps I can take another look at it for myself.' I do not deny that this is a considerable over-simplification of what goes on in a client's mind, but I am quite certain that the intangibles of the relationship bring the final situation about, even after what may be a prolonged period of counselling and by very devious channels. This kind of obscurity was illustrated rather forcibly by one client who had come about some home relationship difficulties, and who during the third meeting was prompted to talk about his interest in art, his ambitions and the frustrations which it caused. For the first time in our meetings he chatted with un-inhibited enjoyment, and quite unexpectedly observed that he now knew how to handle his problem. He departed suddenly, leaving me extremely puzzled, for the discussion about art seemed completely irrelevant. On reflection, however, it occurred to me that simply being interested in what interested him, instead of rejecting it, had enabled him to make his own mind up about something quite different, because no one at home was prepared to talk about his artistic gifts and his feelings about them. Their rejection of his feelings paralysed his ability to maintain harmonious relationships at home. What matters, of course, is that this apparently un-related conversation helped him to act on his own; that I cannot fully understand it is beside the point. Perhaps there was a mechanism inside him which accounted for his behaviour, but it is also true that most of us at some time in our lives have met someone who has influenced, reassured, or inspired us significantly, sometimes long after the meeting and in a similarly inexplicable way. We cannot recall necessarily what was said, but retain the memory of the character and outlook of these other people, the time they gave, the patience they devoted, the clarity of their thinking. Such people have a moral influence stemming from the person and his qualities. So it seems to be with the counsellor.

He may have moral standards of his own, but they are second-ary to his interest in his client; he cares little for the moral image of his activities as viewed by the outsider, for this is overruled by the client's view of him; he has to be as coolly objective as he can, but this is not more important than his client's response to his sensitivity to the latter's feelings; while he is perhaps the main source of strength in the relationship with his client, he presents himself as the instrument through which his clients come to self-realisation and maturity; if he bolsters his client in moments of weakness and anxiety, he does so by questioning these very qualities in order to bring forth the client's strengths: when he gives advice, guidance, information, opinions, he does so because the relationship has made it possible for his client both to seek and to accept it, not because it was imposed at his behest. For tempestuous adolescents, with their transient angers and ephemeral frustrations, this may seem so much high-sounding irrelevance. But they more than anyone need the moral stimulus of someone who is at once at peace with himself yet continually self-critical; who can accept, if need be, the fiery condemnation of a younger generation and face it with a moral challenge to act upon the ideas stated or implied in that condemnation; who can meet the charge of adult self-indulgence with his own dispassionate concern for others. All this comes within the scope of the counselling relationship which abounds in paradoxes and contradictions; perhaps we should not over-indulge ourselves the luxury of searching for any sophisticated explanation or profound moral truths which may lurk behind it. I think it was Sir John Hunt who, on being asked why people climbed Mount Everest, replied: 'Because it is there.' The counsellors' activities may reflect a similarly uncomplicated motive: people are counselled because they exist. Yet even mountains call forth the morality that lies in courage, as well as the intellectual equipment to essay the requisite planning and organisation. So too may counselling evoke the morality which lies in caring for others and the intelligence to arrange it, not to order them about but to develop their own potentialities, however limited these are, and however humble the future tasks of the young clients may be. The alleviation of human unhappiness and misery, of any sort or duration, whether it is real or imagined, by nurturing in the young that sense of responsibility which is most highly developed in man, seems to me to be a moral undertaking. Whether counsellors are conscious of such a moral drive to their work or not is perhaps not of great importance.

This prompts me to end this chapter with a warning to anyone who sees a teacher-counselling service as an outlet for their own conscious urges to do something for others, despite what has been said earlier. Counsellors, whether they work in schools, in social services, in marriage affairs or with young people, whether they are salaried or voluntary, at whatever level of expertise they practise, do not seem consciously to worry much about the motives which drive them onwards, or the nature of any moral principles which sustain them. I have met none who was openly aware of his own virtue, let alone anxious to advertise it. Counsellors believe that they must be as scientific, objective and analytical as they can possibly be, because they must avoid emotional entanglement with their clients: and some of them at least might question my assertion of the need to abandon on occasion the purely scientific component of their activity and method. They would claim that although their ignorance of what makes human beings tick is considerable, even alarming at times, they want and need to know objectively as much as they possibly can about their clients in the sociological, psychological and physiological senses, because only this can really help them to understand their clients, despite the latter's appreciation of the value of the relationship *per se*. The mumbled words of thanks, the occasional letter from a thankful client, almost embarrass them, despite their graceful acceptance of somewhat rare personal acknowledgement of achievements of which they were scarcely aware. But the fact that counsellors are not much preoccupied with the moral basis of their work or the components of their faith does not mean that these do not exist; and the burden of this chapter is that counselling has a moral basis, despite the difficulty of stating it in terms which are clear and tidy and the dangers of formulating it in the language of one religious communion or another, for counsellors' attitudes stretch across the boundaries of religious sects and denominations. All of them, however, are aware that they must at all costs suppress any form of self-gratifying complacency about their competence, and any kind of self-indulgent pleasure at whatever they achieve. Some readers may regard this as a moral attitude in itself.

SUMMARY

The counselling relationship is wholly private to the participants; it is infinitely more complex than the predictable relations between common material substances. It is governed by ascertainable facts and by feelings about those facts, by scientific-objective and non-scientific-subjective considerations. There is a distinction between the caring of the orthodox teacher and the teacher-counsellor, based upon the importance of responsibility in the student, and the counsellor's care is based upon the use of himself and his qualities in what I call relational therapy, while his aim is the restoration of social health. This is a moral purpose; his concern is a moral act; the attributes he uses are moral attributes, and the paradox or duality in counselling disappears in the unity of his moral purpose, because the client's facts and feelings are absorbed into the concern which the counsellor feels. Counsellors, however, are not much concerned, overtly, about their motives and morality, and probably wish to be as objective and factual as possible, because they probably believe that this is the best way of helping clients to what I call social health. Self-satisfaction about their work, or reward for it, are the last considerations in their minds.

VII. Summary and Conclusion

L et me now try to draw together the threads. Although there is some limited experience of personal counselling available in this country, it has hitherto made little impact on education in general. Confusion about its nature undoubtedly exists and this will only disappear as counselling in schools is more widely used. It is concerned with people and their relationships with other people and with their own circumstances; it is not an information service. If we use the term 'guidance' to denote the whole network of services which are at the disposal of young people in schools, personal counselling is a part of it. The starting point of personal counselling is the client and his situation, not what the counsellor may think ought to be done about him or it. It is not a panacea, and no one should infer from my own faith in it that it is a solution for all the highly publicised problems with which schools are and will be faced in the 'sixties and 'seventies of the twentieth century. It is simply one weapon in the armoury of a school. Whether it is the most powerful has yet to be proved.

What is true in this respect of the process of counselling is true also of its practitioners. Personal counsellors are not intended to and cannot replace the normal functions of competent and responsible teachers. Those teachers who undertake home-visiting, organise school social service projects, supervise latecomers, peruse the absence book, undertake careers guidance, provide information about further education, and the other extra-mural tasks which teachers have for long periods undertaken, will not and are not intended to be made superfluous by the existence of a personal counselling service. A counsellor may enable his colleagues to discharge these extra-mural duties more effectively because he possesses skills and attributes which make him a better communicator than many of his colleagues, and thus enable him on occasion to act as a bridge between his clients and his colleagues. But for him to assume a mantle of universal expertise about a wide range of educational tasks which his colleagues perform competently is sheer arrogance: for heads, governors and local authorities to appoint a counsellor with this assumption in view displays only a dangerous ignorance of his true function which is essentially a relation-making and communicating one, and appointing authorities should not be encouraged to think that the manifold sociological problems with which schools are confronted will be solved simply by the establishment and appointment of a counsellor. Moreover it seems to be quite undesirable that anything resembling demarcation lines should be drawn between the function of a counsellor and those of his colleagues who either teach in the purely instructional sense or whose ancillary activities bring them into relationships with their students which closely resemble those created by a counsellor. Herein lie the special advantages of the teacher-counsellor: not only can he talk to his clients as a person, without consideration of age and status, but he can talk to his colleagues as a teacher too. As he accepts his clients, so also must he accept his colleagues. Of course, he will find that some of the latter reject his ideas about relationships with students, because they find them intolerable for reasons which only they can explain, but he will have to work with them harmoniously or at least tolerantly. If, in addition to his skill in communication with clients and colleagues, he can also talk with parents because he is a parent too, then this is an added but not mandatory qualification. But the notion that he, and he alone on the staff, should be the channel through which guidance and communication services should be directed, is not to be encouraged. As his colleagues come to trust his judgement it seems inevitable that they will in fact seek his advice and help about students with whom they form relationships which are significant to the students, but I dislike intensely the prospect that a colleague when approached by a young man seeking some help should say, in effect, 'Do not bother me with this, go and see the counsellor.' The colleague should do what he would have done had there been no counsellor, which is to help in whatever way he can, even if he consults his counselling colleague later about the particular client, and invites his co-operation.

To foster relationships and develop communication, to handle the kind of problems, and to live with the stresses which the teacher-counsellor's duties entail, requires the services of those who are already proven to be first-class teachers of some experience, whose personal qualities are such that they have no need to use traditional authoritarian sanctions in their normal teaching. Their personal qualities are more important than anything else, and I have indicated what these should be. Selection is, therefore, necessary to determine the existence of those personal qualities and must be followed by short but intensive training to condition the selected trainees to the stresses of their new activity. No one should set himself up or be appointed as a counsellor without selection and training. I have rejected the idea of full-time, one year or more examinable courses for four general reasons. The first is that selection is at least as important as training, and that no amount of training can compensate for deficiencies in personal qualities; neither am I convinced of the relevance of an examination. The second is that I have considerable doubts about the benefits which are derivable from the presence in a school of a non-teaching expert, whose occupational separation from contact with his teaching colleagues may increase friction rather than reduce it, because of basic differences in approach, and possible inability to see the point of view of the other person in an argument. The third is that spotlighting counselling as a new-fangled discovery neglects entirely so much about relationships with and guidance for students which has been known to teachers already. The fourth is that I reject the prospect of a lonely expert operating in a school without benefit of guidance by colleagues of a similar outlook and training.

Obviously, then, I am advocating not a new internal specialist skilled in a variety of fields already covered by many competent teachers, but specially orientated teaching members of the staff team, who know where specialised help beyond the capability of themselves and their colleagues can be found, and who can make personal contact with specialists outside the school. The teacher-counsellor system makes possible the existence of two or more such people in a single school, able to co-operate and mutually guide and counsel one another. Moreover, the consequent mini-misation of the gap between teacher-counsellors and teaching colleagues, through those teachers who undertake most compe-tently other forms of guidance work, makes it possible for the counselling approach to penetrate the total staff-student relation-ship within a school. As teachers, including those who have the most dubious views of their counselling colleagues' approach, begin to see the advantages which derive from it, if only measured by the conventional criteria of work and school harmony, so will the techniques of the personal counsellor be appreciated and increasingly adopted. Such a penetration is likely to be a slow process although I can imagine it accelerating as experience grows.

The unique advantage of counselling is that it is always relevant. It will not date or age in the way that syllabuses and teaching techniques do, for any method which is based upon the intrinsic value of people seems to me to be inherently ageless, and applic-able to any imaginable social or historical situation, and counsel-ling is frequently a trouble-avoidance approach to others, as well as a way of helping people to personal harmonisation. It may be argued that this rosy view scarcely applies to the adolescent delin-quents, potential or actual, who seem to trouble our society so much. Some of them may be incurable and socially psychopathic, in which case they are beyond the cure of purely school agencies. I have a sneaking suspicion, however, that schools have more than a little to answer for when it comes to apportioning responsibility for adolescent aggressiveness of one kind or another, at least in the sense of turning their backs upon students who do not measure up to purely intellectual standards or do not choose to conform readily with whatever arbitrary regulations schools impose without either sensible consultation or rational explanation. It is thus not unlikely that the introduction of personal counselling services for the fifteen and upwards age group might contribute much to reducing the incidence of adolescent disturbance and delinquency.

Beyond this I see it as filling a considerable gap between conventional teaching staffs and the outside supporting agencies listed in Appendix II. Too many teachers are unaware of even the existence of at least some of these services, let alone their purposes and locations. Perhaps it is fortunate that they are because some of these agencies are overwhelmed and short-staffed. More significantly these highly trained specialist bodies should be relieved of the burden of cases which a teacher-counsellor could deal with himself, in conjunction with his colleagues or after seeking expert advice from the appropriate service. There are inexhaustible opportunities for team work in this field of personal-relational education: teacher-counsellor with teacher-social worker, teacher-counsellor with school welfare officer, are two examples which spring to mind. One can foresee three or four people co-operating on a particular client, where there are unusually difficult home circumstances. These are imaginary projections into the future perhaps, and for the present we have yet to convince a great many people that the kind of counselling with which I have been concerned is intrinsically right and acceptable, not only to teachers but also to parents and others. And we have a long way to go. A recent conference of schoolteachers in a university was addressed among others by the resident student counsellor, whose exposition of the work was lucid, eloquent and understanding. In later casual conversations with a sizeable sample of the audience,

it was plain that few people had paid much attention to the counsellor's contribution, and that if they had listened they had no
idea at all of what this expert in relational therapy was talking
about or how it satisfied a need in the intellectual development of
the students. I could understand that they did not wish to be
counsellors; what seemed incredible in a well-educated group was
their general inability to appreciate that the counsellor sustained
students in terms of the intellectual progress and fulfilment which
these teachers valued so highly, apart from other accruing benefits.
Fortunately, there are others with less restricted views about
ancillary educational services like counselling; teachers who can
see it as a support to their own particular educational aims; and
parents who regard it not as a substitute for but as a buttress to the
family life and values which they treasure, despite the tribulations
which parents often seem to experience in guiding their children
through adolescence. For counselling – and this needs constant
reiteration to help gain wider acceptance – is not a substitute for
existing teachers nor a replacement for parents. It is a particular
skill, of a relational and communicational kind, based upon the
personal qualities of specially selected teachers, heightened by
training which needs to be almost continuous. Its success and
acceptance by the educational world, by parents and laymen,
depend almost solely upon the demonstrable good faith, sincerity
and character of its practitioners.

This book consists of the thoughts and experiences of one who
found the counselling experience brought to him in his own
teaching career. The suggestions I have made – and they are
scarcely more than the most tentative proposals – for selection,
training and organisation are intended to direct attention to this
new way of helping to make a better job of the whole educational
process than I believe we are making, and not only at the secondary level, but also in further and higher education, where the
need for counselling is at least as great. In economic terms alone
it has prospect of high productivity, to use current jargon; in

personal and social terms I believe the gains could be considerable. This, of course, is a matter of faith, not of objective evidence. What is not a matter of faith, but the observed result of my own not inconsiderable experience with young people of all sorts between the ages of fifteen and twenty-one, is, to quote a letter in *The Times* from the Rev. J. G. Webster, Warden of an East End Glasgow youth club, that 'When these young people are treated as persons by adults who care, then there is a response'. In the quiet privacy of the counselling room in school, meeting on equal terms, the teacher-counsellor can elicit this response from his clients, and it carries over to the world outside and into the future.

Of course, this sounds suspiciously like a soft approach to treatment of adolescents, and there are certainly those who will see in the acceptance principle, as I have outlined it, evidence of that Gadarene slide from the high peaks of traditional social values which is the allegedly fashionable cause of all our adolescent turpitude, real or imagined. The influence of Church and family which I suggested was altering or declining will not, however, be restored by threats of sanctions, of which adolescents are currently oblivious or contemptuous. Neither can the trinity of so-called moral absolutes in human relationships, truth, honesty and goodness, be reinstated – if one accepts that they have disappeared, a contention which I dispute – by authoritarian dictates from any source at all, unless they are accompanied by examples of the sort of conduct which adult society scarcely displays to the adolescents in whom it wishes them to be inculcated. Still less can administrative decrees about raising the school leaving age, or material provision of chromium-plated quasi-mechanical information-dispensers, help society on their own to cope with adolescent needs. They may provide us with better builders, economists and technicians, but they will not necessarily help us to turn out people who can live their lives in some better fashion than the fulfilment of purely personal pleasure and greed.

This, I know, involves us in discussion about the conflict between personal freedom, licence, and the restrictions entailed by living in a society. Some will view counselling, notwithstanding what I have said earlier to the contrary, simply as a peculiarly subtle way of keeping the establishment in business. I, however, have no alternative but to accept that we live in a society which demands adjustments of one sort or another by its individual members. This is part of the context in which I counsel: I cannot run away from it, or turn my back upon it and hope it will disappear, because to do so would not only be a form of self-deception, it would also be a betrayal of my clients, whatever may be my views about the structure of and values displayed by society. If society requires restructuring, because it is in any way wrongly organised, unjust or corrupt, that is a matter for political activists, not counsellors: I am advocating neither the *status quo* nor bloody revolution, only that clients should look searchingly at themselves and their situations. If they want my help, they can have it simply because they are satisfied that I am the sort of person from whom they care to accept it. Thus, those who think that counselling, in Marx's phrase, is a new 'opiate for the masses' are greatly mistaken. Counselling is anything but an opiate: it is a stimulus to examine one's self, an alarming and sometimes painful process, even at the adolescent level, which urges the client to weigh up the pros and cons of his actions *vis-à-vis* others as well as himself.

Counselling, therefore, has nothing to do with the obsolescent debate between the so-called 'hard-liners' and 'soft-liners', between those who contend that students, in school and elsewhere, should do as they are told when they are told without question, and those who think they should do what they like, how they like, when they like, to whomsoever they like. Both extremes are, as likely as not, an escape from the realities of situations with which a personal counsellor has to deal. Advocates of these antithetic positions are unlikely to find counselling attractive for this very reason. What a client does after counselling is for him to decide, but his counselling experience will have given him time and opportunity to evaluate the possible consequences of any decision and action he may take. In the school situation the 'hard-liners' may feel that six of the best to a sixteen-year-old is the best thing for him, and he may think so too, as I have already sugges-ted, because it is quick: but an hour's self-examination may be both more disconcerting and conducive to the growth of responsi-bility. I say 'may' because I do not know what is appropriate for any particular youngster until I have met him, but this has nothing to do with my being a 'hard-liner' or a 'soft-liner'. To those who aver that counselling in a 'tough' school is a weak-kneed ap-proach, I can only say that for some students it may be. I admit that a single counsellor may achieve little, but two counsellors may achieve four times as much as one. I believe that some kind of team operation among the staff may elicit the co-operation of hardened parents, and that concerted efforts by the staff, welfare services and probation officers may achieve miracles. Given time, patience and hope, such efforts may keep someone out of gaol in the long run. And this is a considerable achievement in purely economic terms as well as social. But if the critics have no faith in such personal-orientated measures, with individuals or small groups, they should not try them, for faith is what they will need, especially at first.

Neither is counselling psychiatry on the cheap. I do not pretend to cope with the mentally sick, although I hope to be able to recognise symptoms in a client which will make me look at his normal school records and any other information on which I can lay my hands, and then seek counsel myself from experts, before referring him to them with a lucid report to justify my suspicions. I am not advocating that I can cure my clients or condition them by some form of clinical therapy which is beyond my capability and therefore dangerous for me to essay. Nor do I look for 'nut-cases'. My clients have been suffering from loneliness, anger, rejection, frustration, anxiety, sadness – the sort of personal-social maladies which plague thousands of adults, and, like the adults, complicated by that chronic loneliness which is the endemic social disease of our time and for all generations, despite a plethora of officially established social agencies. Drugs, pep pills, alcohol, even excessive sexual indulgence, are ways to oblivious escape from the symptoms, not a cure for the absence of someone to talk to. For the latter is often the counsellor's job, and if it seems a trivial task, we might well ponder how often each of us has wanted to tell someone something, not because they could do anything about it, but because there was some compulsion within us to unburden ourselves of ideas and views, good or bad, as a means of relieving tension which could otherwise manifest itself, perhaps in anti-social activity. The mother who says, 'Not now, dear, I'm cooking the dinner'; the father who says, 'Sorry, lad, I'm meeting George at the pub'; the teacher who is preoccupied with marking books, when ten minutes of time may be extremely significant to the youngster who wants to say or ask something which is important to him, all provide business for the counsellor. He has to shoulder a burden which perhaps should not be his; but he or the kind of team-counselling I have suggested may be able to put it back in its proper place, and thus prevent the growth of loneliness-rejection syndromes into real social and psychological disturbance.

Of course, this book is full of 'mights' and 'mays', or 'perhaps' and 'possibly', for no other reason than that counselling is new, its results uncertain, and that 'social disease' and 'personal therapy' are unfamiliar concepts, at least to the teaching world. Thirty years of teaching and a less experience of counselling has made me sure of two things only: that I know very little about what makes human beings tick, and that they have to be seen and considered in relation to a constantly changing contemporary social background. Counselling is not conjuring or magic, form-filling or computerised measurement; it is not slick, clever, efficient or accurate. It is about people, whose problems are most often not material but personal and moral, and always urgent. Its roots must lie in dispassionate concern and disinterested sympathy, in care for others. These comprise the moral ground on which it is based. Its moral function is to hold out a hand to anyone who is struggling in the pool of life, to elicit from them the response of which the Glasgow Club Warden wrote. It is not a function of business-like experts appointed to schools to discharge an army of functions for a host of people: a duty beyond the capacity of a single person, and which is more likely to drive him to exhaustion than anything else. It is not a service to be swept into a tidy and administrative machine with periods for counselling in the time-table. It is not a new-fangled fashion to be worn in the enthusiasm of the moment. It is, so far, a somewhat untidy way of bringing some peace of mind to some young people in schools and in colleges and universities, and perhaps getting more out of them than they or the counsellors believed possible, because it is founded upon a humble concern for people and an explicit faith in their value and meaning.

Professor Margaret Robinson,* of Oregon, United States, made a plea at the 1968 International Congress on Mental Health for closer relationships between teachers and pupils. A lack of communication between teacher and pupil, she said, tended to breed rebellion, indifference, truancy and a distaste for academic knowledge. But an inspiring teacher could have a profound posi-tive effect upon the personalities of his pupils. She continued, 'The pulse of our youth beats a haunting plea for a world with real people who mean what they say, who are free from façades, who believe in what they do, and who are genuine.' Counselling in schools by teachers seems to be at least part of the answer to these pleas, and more teachers might, moreover, find counselling rewarding. They should therefore consider acquainting them-selves with this essentially human art of eliciting responses from

* Reported in *The Times*, August 14th 1968.

their youthful clients and responding sincerely to their clients' thoughts. They will, however, be wise to remember that to do so demands on the counsellor's side a continuous and searching examination of his own ideas and attitudes, a process of which selection and training are an inescapable part.

APPENDIX I

Further Reading

The following suggestions do not constitute an exhaustive list, but they are a representative selection of relevant background books. They are arranged under certain headings, but many of them include matter which falls within the purview of others.

DEVELOPMENT AND PSYCHOLOGY

The Development of Personality: T. A. Ratcliffe (National Marriage Guidance Council, London 1961)

Childhood and Adolescence: J. A. Hadfield (Pelican, Harmondsworth 1965)

The Physiology of Sex: K. Walker (Pelican, Harmondsworth 1964)

Journey Through Adolescence: D. Odlum (Penguin, Harmondsworth 1962)

Psychology for Ministers and Social Workers: H. Guntripp (Independent Press, London 1963)

SOCIAL AND FAMILY

The Insecure Offenders: T. R. Fyvel (Penguin, Harmondsworth 1963)

Youth and the Social Order: F. Musgrove (Routledge and Kegan Paul, London 1964)

The Family and Marriage: R. Fletcher (Penguin, Harmondsworth 1962)

The Child, the Family and the Outside World: D.W. Winnicott (Pelican, Harmondsworth 1962)

MORALITY AND ETHICS

Moral Education in a Changing World: Ed. W. R. Niblett (Faber & Faber, London 1965)

Personal Values in the Modern World: M. O. V. Jeffreys (Pelican, Harmondsworth 1963)

Sex and Society: P. Fletcher and K. Walker (Pelican, Harmondsworth 1964)

The Faith of the Counsellors: P. Halmos (Constable, London 1965)

Morals in a Free Society: M. Kelling (S.C.M. Press, London 1967)

Sex and Teenagers in Love: L. Barnett (Denholm House Press, Redhill 1968)

Introduction to Moral Education: J. Wilson, N. Williams and B. Sugarman (Pelican, Harmondsworth 1967)

Marriage Guidance: The Journal of the National Marriage Guidance Council, published in alternate months, contains articles, comments and reviews of great interest to teachers, as well as other material.

OFFICIAL REPORTS

Half Our Future: (The Newsom Report) (H.M.S.O. 1963)

Counselling in Schools*: (Working Paper No. 15); Schools Council (H.M.S.O. 1967)

Sex Education in Schools†: (Birmingham Education Committee 1967)

Education for Personal Relationships and Family Life†: (Gloucestershire Education Committee 1966)

---

* The only publication dealing specifically with counselling in schools in this country.
   † These were referred to in discussing selection and training.

APPENDIX II

Agencies and Services which may assist a Counsellor

Some teachers are very well acquainted with social service agencies, both statutory and voluntary, which can be useful to them; others do not even know of their existence. The former will find the following list and accompanying notes inadequate, or indeed misleading, in the light of their detailed knowledge of their local situation; the latter should treat the list with care, use it simply as a guide to what may be available in their own locality, and find out for themselves exactly what is available and where. Having done this they should then try to make personal contact with someone in the services which are most commonly used. While there is a certain uniformity about the title of local authority and statutory services maintained out of public funds, there are local variations in the names of local voluntary social services and the precise functions they discharge. Local Councils of Social Service, or Citizens' Advice Bureaux can often be extremely helpful in providing such information.

I take this further opportunity of reminding school counsellors of any sort that they should not initiate action with any supporting agency without obtaining the client's agreement, and if it is at all possible, the consent of his family as well. Matters which a counsellor may think require better help than he can give frequently involve the family of the youngster concerned. They will usually be glad to have an offer of help, but this must never be assumed.

The following list is not necessarily exhaustive and the brief notes are only a guide to their functions, not comprehensive descriptions. Many of them are seriously overloaded, and may be glad to guide the counsellor rather than take a given case over.

I. AGENCIES AVAILABLE THROUGH THE LOCAL EDUCATION OFFICE
School Welfare Officers: can give much useful information about home conditions.
School Medical Department: through its nurses can also provide informa-

tion about home and family health problems.

Child Guidance Department: providers of expert advice on child behaviour.

Children's Department: concerned with child care and deprivation.

Youth Employment Department: The contact in school should be the Careers Master(s), and counsellors should work through the latter if careers problems arise in counselling.

Youth Service and Community Service: can give information about opportunities for involvement in youth work or community service.

Probation Service: can give excellent advice about adolescents, and home and neighbourhood influence. Consulting this service does not mean that a client will finish up in court.

2. OTHER AGENCIES

Moral Welfare: Local arrangements for Moral Welfare should be ascertained, as religious affiliations of particular clients' families are involved: they can give professional guidance in, for example, pregnancy.

Family Service Units; Personal Service Societies; Family Welfare Services: are all concerned with help to families either as part of their total function or as their specific purpose. Local arrangements should be ascertained.

NSPCC: experts in matters of neglect of or cruelty to children.

APPENDIX III

Educational Institutions offering Counselling Courses; or courses in Careers Guidance, Social Work and Youth Service which contain a counselling element

University of Keele, Institute of Education
University of Reading, Institute of Education
University of Exeter, Institute of Education
University of Leeds, Institute of Education
University of Manchester, Department of Education
University of Manchester, Department of Social Administration

Tavistock Institute of Human Relations, London

Chelsea College of Physical Education, Eastbourne
Culham College, Abingdon, Berks
Dartford College of Physical Education, Kent
Edge Hill College of Education, Ormskirk, Lancs
Kenton College of Education, Newcastle-on-Tyne
Kesteven Training College, Lincs
Notre Dame College of Education, Liverpool
Newland Park Training College, Bucks
City of Portsmouth College of Education
Swansea College of Education
Westhill Training College, Birmingham

Details of the Courses offered by individual institutions can be obtained direct from the institutions themselves, as course contents are likely to vary from year to year.

Index